SCHOLASTIC

W9-APL-620

Daily Trait Warm-Ups

180 Revision and Editing Activities to Kick Off Writing Time

Ruth Culham

NEW YORK • TORONTO • LONDON • AUCKLAND • SYDNEY
MEXICO CITY • NEW DELHI • HONG KONG • BUENOS AIRES

Teaching *Resources*

To the Scholastic Teaching Resources team,

who believed—from the beginning—

that this work would help teachers and students.

Editors: Joanna Davis-Swing, Sarah Longhi, and Raymond Coutu
Interior Design: Solas
Cover Designer: Ka-Yeon Kim
Copy Editor: Erich Strom

ISBN-13: 978-0-545-09599-0
ISBN-10: 0-545-09599-9

1 2 3 4 5 6 7 8 9 10 40 14 13 12 11 10 09

Contents

 # Introduction

It's hard to imagine a teacher's day getting any busier. With classrooms loaded to the windowsills with children, challenging performance standards, and an ever-expanding curriculum, it's no wonder teachers often ask, "How am I going to get all of this done?" especially when it comes to teaching writing.

Teaching writing has always been a time-consuming task. After all, it's about learning to think clearly and transform that thinking into clearly composed text. There are no shortcuts for that. But over the years, as the traits of writing, which are listed in the box below, have been woven into the writing classroom, teachers have found ingenious ways to do more with less time.

> **IDEAS:** the meaning and development of the message
>
> **ORGANIZATION:** the internal structure of the piece
>
> **VOICE:** the tone of the piece—the personal stamp of the writer
>
> **WORD CHOICE:** the vocabulary the writer uses to convey meaning
>
> **SENTENCE FLUENCY:** the rhythm and flow of words and phrases
>
> **CONVENTIONS:** the mechanical correctness of the piece

Aligning the traits of writing with the revision and editing processes has been an important breakthrough. Finally, we have a way to show students not only what to revise and edit, but *how* to revise and edit. Finally, students are successfully managing these complex processes for themselves. Finally, thanks to the traits and excellent instruction, teachers at every grade level are seeing student writing performance soar. (For background information on the traits, see page 7.) As such, I've organized this book into two sections:

- Revision, which covers traits that help students draft and refine their work: ideas, organization, voice, word choice, and sentence fluency
- Editing, which covers the trait that ensures that their work adheres to English-language standards: conventions

Within each section, I offer reproducible warm-up activities designed to give your students focused writing practice. The warm-ups in the revision section are organized around small subsets, or key qualities, of each trait, making the trait more manageable for you to teach and for students to learn.

Key Qualities of the Revision Traits

Ideas
Finding a Topic
Focusing the Topic
Developing the Topic
Using Details

Organization
Creating the Lead
Using Sequence Words
Developing the Body
Ending With a Sense of Resolution

Voice
Establishing a Tone
Conveying the Purpose
Creating a Connection to the Audience
Taking Risks to Create Voice

Word Choice
Using Strong Verbs
Using Striking Words and Phrases
Using Words That Are Specific
    and Accurate
Using Language Effectively

Sentence Fluency
Crafting Well-Built Sentences
Varying Sentence Patterns
Breaking the "Rules" to Create Fluency
Capturing Smooth and Rhythmic Flow

You can distribute photocopies of the warm-ups so students can work on them on their own or in small groups, or you can make them into transparencies to use with an overhead projector and revise and edit them with the whole class. You can also use the enclosed CD, which contains all the warm-ups in the book, to project or print paper copies for students or project-specific pages for the whole class. Sample responses and answers are provided at the back of the book.

In addition, each key quality has a "Think About" section, which you can use to help students focus on important questions about a trait as they write. For example, the Think About for using sequence words for sentence fluency consists of the following questions:

- Have I used order words like *first, next, then,* and *finally*?

- Did I use a variety of transition words like *however, because, also,* and *for instance*?

- Have I shown how ideas connect from sentence to sentence?

- Does my organization make sense from paragraph to paragraph?

Like the warm-ups, you can print or project the Think Abouts from the enclosed CD. Or, if you wish, you can make photocopies or overhead transparencies directly from this book.

By focusing on key qualities, students learn the language of the traits and the power the traits bring to their writing. In the process, they learn how writing works, which allows us to teach more deeply, efficiently, and supportively. (For more suggestions on how to use this book, see pages 8–9.)

Learning how to revise and edit may be challenging for young writers, but it can also be enjoyable. These warm-ups are designed to provide meaningful guided practice and to cover topics that are of interest to students in grades 3 and up, so they're both effective and engaging. Whether you are teaching students how to clarify their writing through revision, clean up their writing through editing, or both, these practical, ready-to-use activities will help.

Some Background on the Traits of Writing Model

It's been about 20 years since the traits of writing were conceived and incorporated into the lexicons of writing teachers and students. I feel privileged to have been there right at the beginning—first as a teacher, and then as a researcher at the Northwest Regional Educational Laboratory, where the traits of writing model was refined and launched nationally. Now, as a writer with my own company devoted to conducting workshops and developing writing resources for teachers and students, I enjoy working with teachers across the country and all over the world as they embrace the model for assessment and instruction. I have seen firsthand the huge, positive influence the traits have had on students and teachers in writing classrooms everywhere.

Using the language of the traits empowers students and teachers to identify the qualities they see in writing and communicate clearly about them. As a backbone for this critical communication, the traits are dynamic, thoughtful, and nonprescriptive.

We use trait terminology consistently, from teacher to teacher and from year to year, to build our understanding of what good writing looks like and to help students generate texts that exceed our wildest expectations. Using the traits for assessment and instruction links these two vital processes in specific and meaningful ways. We assess students' writing to find out what they know and can do; then, we use our assessments to focus writing instruction on areas where students need the most work. It's a powerful combination—assessment and instruction. The traits make that connection easy to understand and even easier to implement in today's writing classroom.

How to Use This Book

As mentioned earlier, in this book you will find warm-up activities for each trait, along with directions on how to carry them out. For the ideas, organization, voice, word choice, and sentence fluency traits, the warm-ups center on developing critical revision skills. For the conventions trait, they help build editing skills in spelling, punctuation, capitalization, paragraphing, and grammar and usage. At the back of the book you'll find "answers" for, or corrected versions of, the editing warm-ups and sample responses for the revision warm-ups (since there's no single correct way to revise a piece of writing). You can use the sample responses with students or create your own as you go.

I've provided enough warm-ups for them to be used on a daily basis—one for each of 180 school days. But that doesn't mean you need to use them sequentially. You should use them in whatever order you wish. The important thing is to use them in a way that makes sense for you and your students and to make sure that you cover them all by the year's end. You may first want to assess your students' writing using the trait scoring guides found in my book *6+1 Traits of Writing: The Complete Guide for Grades 3 and Up* (Scholastic, 2003). Doing so may highlight specific traits that your students struggle with most.

You can complete specific warm-ups with the whole class, using a traditional overhead projector or a digital projector. Students can follow along and complete the warm-ups with you or complete them on their own or with a partner. The warm-ups require original writing—an improvement over traditional worksheet practice. You may wish to distribute copies of the Think About that accompanies each warm-up so students can use it to guide their revision and editing. These Think Abouts come in handy on *all* writing projects, not just warm-ups, so encourage students to keep them in their notebooks for easy reference.

It's vital to work the warm-ups into your own classroom writing routines, but here is one suggestion for getting started:

1. Project or give students a copy of the Think About for the warm-up you're working on.

2. Briefly discuss the Think About so students understand the trait's key quality and the questions they should be asking themselves as they write.

3. Project or give students a copy of the warm-up activity. Ask students to complete it by themselves or with a partner. Responses will vary because students are expected to revise the warm-up text, not just fill in right answers.

4. Write your own response and share it with students. If you like, you can use the sample responses to revision warm-ups or answers to editing warm-ups included at the back of the book.

5. Allow students to share their responses and discuss.

6. If time allows, encourage students to choose pieces from their writing folders to revise or edit using the same trait and Think About questions. Linking warm-ups to their own work provides practice and builds independence.

I've also included student-friendly scoring guides for each trait so students can easily assess their own work as they write and look for places to revise and edit. These scoring guides can be used in conjunction with the revision checklist (page 116) and the list of editor's marks (page 119), which contain handy reminders of things all writers need to think about as they draft and polish their work.

Regardless of how you carry out the warm-ups, students should take what they learn and apply it to their own extended pieces that they create during writing time—pieces that come from your curriculum and grade-level units of study. Since students are working on these pieces over time, they can apply what they learn about revision and editing as they learn it. The result is final pieces that are thoughtful and polished. Having students revise and edit their own work using the language of the traits is critical to helping them understand how and when to revise and edit, regardless of the purpose for their writing. The sooner students understand and begin using the tools that successful, independent writers use to improve their work, the sooner they'll become successful, independent writers themselves.

PART I

Revision Warm-Ups

Revision is the stage in the writing process where writers look and relook at their piece, checking for logic, clarity, and cohesiveness. Revision literally means "seeing again." To make their writing as clear as possible, writers need to learn how to see what is working and what isn't. From there, they can rework the text, based on what they feel it needs in order to meet their purpose for writing it and satisfy their audience. Often, however, as most teachers know, students struggle with this stage or skip it altogether. They are not sure how to make the idea clear, create an organization that flows, use a voice that is appropriate for the audience, select "just-right" words or phrases, or come up with sentences that sing. But for writing to work, young writers need to be able to do all of these things. Our task as their teachers is to show them how.

This is exactly why the traits are so powerful. They enable us to show students how to break down their writing into manageable parts and focus their attention on building skills.

The warm-ups in this section focus on the first five traits: ideas, organization, voice, word choice, and sentence fluency. Each trait is broken down into four key qualities, with warm-ups that address each quality. For example, for the ideas trait, students practice (1) finding a topic, (2) focusing the topic, (3) developing the topic, and (4) using details. Each set of warm-ups has its own Think About, which contains questions to help students as they revise. By the time students have finished working with these warm-ups, they will have developed a significant number of important revision skills—skills that can be applied every time they write, whether they're writing fiction or nonfiction.

Follow the directions at the top of each page. Use the suggested responses in the back if you wish, or write your own. It's just that easy to begin demystifying the process of revision for you and your students.

IDEAS

KEY QUALITIES

Finding a Topic

Focusing the Topic

Developing the Topic

Using Details

Think ABOUT

FINDING A TOPIC

- Have I chosen a topic that I really like?

- Do I have something new to say about this topic?

- Am I writing about what I know and care about?

- Have I gathered enough information so that I'm ready to write?

 **Finding a Topic**

Read this example:

There are many kinds of people in the world. Little brothers can be so irritating sometimes. Adults and kids like different things.

Choose a topic from the example. Write a draft using details that make the topic clear.

_____

_____

_____

_____

_____

_____

_____

_____

Think ABOUT

- Have I chosen a topic that I really like?

- Do I have something new to say about this topic?

- Am I writing about what I know and care about?

- Have I gathered enough information so that I'm ready to write?

See the sample response, page 183.

 **Finding a Topic**

Read this example:

Mount Rushmore is the most awesome of all the national monuments. The United States has 50 states. There are many rivers and lakes across the United States.

Choose a topic from the example. Write a draft using details that make the topic clear.

_____

_____

_____

_____

_____

_____

_____

_____

Think ABOUT

- Have I chosen a topic that I really like?

- Do I have something new to say about this topic?

- Am I writing about what I know and care about?

- Have I gathered enough information so that I'm ready to write?

See the sample response, page 183.

⚡ Finding a Topic

Read this example:

> **I'd rather cook than eat out at a restaurant. I like to watch cooking shows on TV. The cake I made for my brother's birthday was not pretty, but it sure did taste good.**

Choose a topic from the example. Write a draft using details that make the topic clear.

_____

_____

_____

_____

_____

_____

_____

Think ABOUT

- Have I chosen a topic that I really like?

- Do I have something new to say about this topic?

- Am I writing about what I know and care about?

- Have I gathered enough information so that I'm ready to write?

See the sample response, page 183.

Finding a Topic

1. Read this example:

Last Monday was the worst day of my life. I wonder why Pluto is no longer listed as a major planet. My new backpack is a lot more comfortable than my old one. My soccer team is going to be awesome this year. Do you prefer bananas when they are green and firm or ripe and squishy?

2. Revise it on a separate sheet of paper, using the Think About questions to select a topic and generate details that describe it well.

Think ABOUT

- Have I chosen a topic that I really like?

- Do I have something new to say about this topic?

- Am I writing about what I know and care about?

- Have I gathered enough information so that I'm ready to write?

3. Use the student-friendly scoring guide to score your writing:

1 2 3 4 5

See the sample response, page 183, and the student-friendly scoring guide, page 31.

IDEAS

Think ABOUT

FOCUSING THE TOPIC

- Have I zeroed in on one small part of a bigger idea?

- Can I tell you my idea in a simple sentence?

- Have I chosen the information that matches my idea best?

- Have I thought about what the reader will need to know?

 **Focusing the Topic**

Revise this example:

> **It can be scary to be left on your own. My parents leave me home sometimes when they go out to the movies. None of my brothers or sisters mind being alone in the house.**

Concentrate on focusing the topic to create a more detailed draft.

_____

_____

_____

_____

_____

_____

_____

_____

Think ABOUT

- Have I zeroed in on one small part of a bigger idea?
- Can I tell you my idea in a simple sentence?
- Have I chosen the information that matches my idea best?
- Have I thought about what the reader will need to know?

See the sample response, page 183.

 **Focusing the Topic**

Revise this example:

I enjoy looking at fine art. Vincent van Gogh is a famous painter. Museums are trying to encourage more people of all ages to come and visit.

Concentrate on focusing the topic to create a more detailed draft.

_____

_____

_____

_____

_____

_____

_____

Think ABOUT

- Have I zeroed in on one small part of a bigger idea?

- Can I tell you my idea in a simple sentence?

- Have I chosen the information that matches my idea best?

- Have I thought about what the reader will need to know?

See the sample response, page 183.

 **Focusing the Topic**

Revise this example:

The news article explained the role of rain forests in our environment. My family and I went to Brazil to visit a rain forest. The rain forests are disappearing at an alarming rate.

Concentrate on focusing the topic to create a more detailed draft.

_____

_____

_____

_____

_____

_____

_____

Think ABOUT

- Have I zeroed in on one small part of a bigger idea?
- Can I tell you my idea in a simple sentence?
- Have I chosen the information that matches my idea best?
- Have I thought about what the reader will need to know?

See the sample response, page 183.

 **Focusing the Topic**

1. Read this example:

> **Pluto was discovered in 1930. It is made of ice and rock. The other planets are Mercury, Venus, Earth, Mars, Jupiter, Saturn, Uranus, and Neptune. Venus is my favorite planet other than Earth. Pluto is now called a "dwarf planet." Some planets have moons. Pluto's orbit goes inside the orbit of Neptune. No other planet's orbit does this. The International Astronomical Union decided in August 2006 not to list Pluto as a major planet anymore.**

2. Revise it on a separate sheet of paper, using the Think About questions to narrow the piece down to one aspect of the main idea and add details to develop that aspect.

Think ABOUT

- Have I zeroed in on one small part of a bigger idea?
- Can I tell you my idea in a simple sentence?
- Have I chosen the information that matches my idea best?
- Have I thought about what the reader will need to know?

3. Use the student-friendly scoring guide to score your writing:

1 2 3 4 5

See the sample response, page 183, and the student-friendly scoring guide, page 31.

IDEAS

Think ABOUT

DEVELOPING THE TOPIC

- Am I sure my information is right?

- Are my details chock-full of interesting information?

- Have I used details that show new thinking about this idea?

- Will the reader believe what I say about this topic?

Developing the Topic

Revise this example:

Summer vacation is fun. When summer comes, I like to play outside, but I don't like to do chores.

Develop this topic with interesting, accurate information.

_____

_____

_____

_____

_____

_____

_____

_____

Think ABOUT

- Am I sure my information is right?
- Are my details chock-full of interesting information?
- Have I used details that show new thinking about this idea?
- Will the reader believe what I say about this topic?

See the sample response, page 183.

 **Developing the Topic**

Revise this example:

Have you ever been around cows? My brother is scared of them. I tried to tip a cow once.

Develop this topic with interesting, accurate information.

_____

_____

_____

_____

_____

_____

_____

_____

Think ABOUT

- Am I sure my information is right?
- Are my details chock-full of interesting information?
- Have I used details that show new thinking about this idea?
- Will the reader believe what I say about this topic?

See the sample response, page 183.

 **Developing the Topic**

Revise this example:

Rain is wet and cold. It's not much fun on a rainy day. Rainy days are boring.

Develop this topic with interesting, accurate information.

_____

_____

_____

_____

_____

_____

_____

_____

Think ABOUT

- Am I sure my information is right?
- Are my details chock-full of interesting information?
- Have I used details that show new thinking about this idea?
- Will the reader believe what I say about this topic?

See the sample response, page 184.

 **Developing the Topic**

1. Read this example:

Pluto is a huge planet. It takes 538 years for Pluto to orbit the sun. It was discovered in 1980 and named after Aristotle Pluto, the famous astronomer. There have been three trips to Pluto, and there are plans to have even more space trips there in the future. It's very hot on Pluto, almost as hot as the sun. The color of Pluto is greenish purple, and you can spot it easily in the night sky.

2. Revise it on a separate sheet of paper, using the Think About questions to make sure the details are all correct and make sense. (You may want to check an encyclopedia or reliable Web site.)

Think ABOUT

- Am I sure my information is right?

- Are my details chock-full of interesting information?

- Have I used details that show new thinking about this idea?

- Will the reader believe what I say about this topic?

3. Use the student-friendly scoring guide to score your writing:

1 2 3 4 5

See the sample response, page 184, and the student-friendly scoring guide, page 31.

IDEAS

Think ABOUT

USING DETAILS

- Did I create a picture in the reader's mind?

- Did I use details that draw upon the five senses? (sight, touch, taste, smell, hearing)

- Do my details stay on the main topic?

- Did I stretch for details beyond the obvious?

 **Using Details**

Revise this example:

I found a seashell at the beach. I found some rocks and sea glass at the beach. I looked at tide pools at the beach.

Use details to make the idea crystal clear.

_____

_____

_____

_____

_____

_____

_____

_____

_____

Think ABOUT

- Did I create a picture in the reader's mind?

- Did I use details that draw upon the five senses? (sight, touch, taste, smell, hearing)

- Do my details stay on the main topic?

- Did I stretch for details beyond the obvious?

See the sample response, page 184.

☼ Using Details

Revise this example:

Hurricane season happens once a year or so. Hurricanes do a lot of damage. Hurricanes have strong winds and can damage buildings and homes.

Use details to make the idea crystal clear.

_____

_____

_____

_____

_____

_____

_____

Think ABOUT

- Did I create a picture in the reader's mind?
- Did I use details that draw upon the five senses? (sight, touch, taste, smell, hearing)
- Do my details stay on the main topic?
- Did I stretch for details beyond the obvious?

See the sample response, page 184.

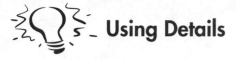 **Using Details**

Revise this example:

I thought I heard someone following me when I walked home. But when I turned around, I saw that it was my neighbor's dog.

Use details to make the idea crystal clear.

_____

_____

_____

_____

_____

_____

_____

_____

Think ABOUT

- Did I create a picture in the reader's mind?

- Did I use details that draw upon the five senses? (sight, touch, taste, smell, hearing)

- Do my details stay on the main topic?

- Did I stretch for details beyond the obvious?

See the sample response, page 184.

Using Details

1. Read this example:

> **Pluto is very small. It's very, very cold. It's very, very far away. Pluto was the ninth planet. Neptune and Jupiter are other planets. Now they say it's not big enough to be called a planet anymore. There are other reasons, too, like it hasn't cleared its own orbit and the other planets have. They've been arguing about it since 1930.**

2. Revise it on a separate sheet of paper, using the Think About questions to help you include details that will make the topic clearer for the reader. (You may want to check an encyclopedia or reliable Web site.)

Think ABOUT

- Did I create a picture in the reader's mind?
- Did I use details that draw upon the five senses? (sight, touch, taste, smell, hearing)
- Do my details stay on the main topic?
- Did I stretch for details beyond the obvious?

3. Use the student-friendly scoring guide to score your writing:

1 2 3 4 5

See the sample response, page 184, and the student-friendly scoring guide, page 31.

Ideas

The Meaning and Development of the Message

Student-Friendly Scoring Guide

It all makes sense.

My reader will learn a lot.

It's really clear.

5 Ready to share!

This is just what I wanted to say.

Good, juicy details!

4

My reader might have some questions.

It TELLS, but it doesn't SHOW very clearly.

My reader will get the general idea.

I need to add some details.

I'm working on it!

Halfway home!

3

2

Just beginning

I'm afraid my reader won't follow this.

It's hard to get started.

I'm not sure what my topic is . . . or maybe my topic is too BIG.

The picture is not very clear.

I need more time to think.

1

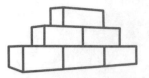

ORGANIZATION

Think ABOUT

CREATING THE LEAD

- Did I give the reader something interesting to think about right from the start?

- Will the reader want to keep reading?

- Have I tried to get the reader's attention?

- Did I let the reader know what is coming?

🧱 Creating the Lead

Revise this example:

My name is Devon and I'm going to tell you about a time I went fishing. I went fishing one day last summer. It's a lot of fun to go fishing.

Write a lead that informs and "hooks" your reader.

_____

_____

_____

_____

_____

_____

_____

Think ABOUT

- Did I give the reader something interesting to think about right from the start?

- Will the reader want to keep reading?

- Have I tried to get the reader's attention?

- Did I let the reader know what is coming?

See the sample response, page 184.

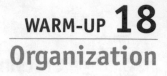

Creating the Lead

Revise this example:

I like reality shows. I think everyone should watch them. What they show is always unexpected.

Write a lead that informs and "hooks" your reader.

_____

_____

_____

_____

_____

_____

_____

_____

Think ABOUT

- Did I give the reader something interesting to think about right from the start?

- Will the reader want to keep reading?

- Have I tried to get the reader's attention?

- Did I let the reader know what is coming?

See the sample response, page 184.

 **Creating the Lead**

Revise this example:

> **This paper is about kids deciding for themselves when to go to bed. I think kids should choose their own bedtimes. Should kids get to set their own bedtimes?**

Write a lead that informs and "hooks" your reader.

_____

_____

_____

_____

_____

_____

_____

Think ABOUT

- Did I give the reader something interesting to think about right from the start?

- Will the reader want to keep reading?

- Have I tried to get the reader's attention?

- Did I let the reader know what is coming?

See the sample response, page 184.

Creating the Lead

1. Read this example:

I'm going to tell you three things about my terrible day last Monday. It was an awful day. Everything I said made people mad and everything I did turned out badly. I was also grouchy. I wonder why some days are like that? I wish I could go back in time and redo last Monday. It was a terrible, terrible day.

2. Revise it on a separate sheet of paper, using the Think About questions to write a new lead sentence that will really get the reader's attention. Add interesting details to the body.

Think ABOUT

- Did I give the reader something interesting to think about right from the start?

- Will the reader want to keep reading?

- Have I tried to get the reader's attention?

- Did I let the reader know what is coming?

3. Use the student-friendly scoring guide to score your writing:

1 2 3 4 5

See the sample response, page 184, and the student-friendly scoring guide, page 52.

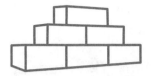

ORGANIZATION

Think ABOUT

USING SEQUENCE WORDS

- Have I used order words like *first*, *next*, *then*, and *finally*?

- Did I use a variety of transition words like *however*, *because*, *also*, and *for instance*?

- Have I shown how ideas connect from sentence to sentence?

- Does my organization make sense from paragraph to paragraph?

Using Sequence Words

Revise this example:

It started to rain. We got soaked. We ran into the building. The thunder and lightning lasted for hours.

Use sequence words to show the order of your ideas. Add details if you wish.

_____

_____

_____

_____

_____

_____

_____

_____

Think ABOUT

- Have I used order words like *first, next, then,* and *finally?*

- Did I use a variety of transition words like *however, because, also,* and *for instance?*

- Have I shown how ideas connect from sentence to sentence?

- Does my organization make sense from paragraph to paragraph?

See the sample response, page 185.

 **Using Sequence Words**

Revise this example:

> **I opened the package. I poured out the cake mix. I cracked open an egg. I added water. I mixed the ingredients together. I poured the mix into a pan. I baked the cake.**

Use sequence words to show the order of your ideas. Add details if you wish.

_____

_____

_____

_____

_____

_____

_____

Think ABOUT

- Have I used order words like *first*, *next*, *then*, and *finally*?

- Did I use a variety of transition words like *however*, *because*, *also*, and *for instance*?

- Have I shown how ideas connect from sentence to sentence?

- Does my organization make sense from paragraph to paragraph?

See the sample response, page 185.

Using Sequence Words

Revise this example:

I wrote my story. I reread it. I found some mistakes. I changed the story to make it stronger. I read it to a friend. I proofread it. I published my story.

Use sequence words to show the order of your ideas. Add details if you wish.

_____

_____

_____

_____

_____

_____

_____

Think ABOUT

- Have I used order words like *first, next, then,* and *finally?*

- Did I use a variety of transition words like *however, because, also,* and *for instance?*

- Have I shown how ideas connect from sentence to sentence?

- Does my organization make sense from paragraph to paragraph?

See the sample response, page 185.

 **Using Sequence Words**

1. Read this example and underline the sequence words:

> **Finally, the day was over. Do you ever have days when you wish you hadn't ever gotten out of bed? That's how my day was last Monday. I was happy to have a chance at a better day on Tuesday. Another thing that was upsetting was my dog ran after the neighbor's cat and Mrs. Kuvluc yelled at poor Marco. At first I thought I was just in a lousy mood and that's why bad things kept happening. But then my bad mood spilled over to my mom when I didn't like the breakfast she made me and it hurt her feelings.**

2. Revise it on a separate sheet of paper, using the Think About questions to put all the information in the right order.

Think ABOUT

- Have I used order words like *first*, *next*, *then*, and *finally*?
- Did I use a variety of transition words like *however*, *because*, *also*, and *for instance*?
- Have I shown how ideas connect from sentence to sentence?
- Does my organization make sense from paragraph to paragraph?

3. Use the student-friendly scoring guide to score your writing:

1 2 3 4 5

See the sample response, page 185, and the student-friendly scoring guide, page 52.

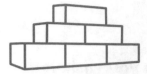

ORGANIZATION

Think ABOUT

DEVELOPING THE BODY

- Have I shown the reader where to slow down and where to speed up?

- Do all the details fit where they are placed?

- Will the reader find it easy to follow my ideas?

- Does the organization help the main idea stand out?

 **Developing the Body**

Revise this example:

The boxes were everywhere. We loaded them onto the truck. My mom told me we were going to move. I wrapped my trophies carefully so they wouldn't break. It was hard saying good-bye to my friends.

Develop the body by putting details in the right place to guide your reader. Apply all your organization skills, including using sequence words.

_____

_____

_____

_____

_____

_____

_____

_____

Think ABOUT

- Have I shown the reader where to slow down and where to speed up?

- Do all the details fit where they are placed?

- Will the reader find it easy to follow my ideas?

- Does the organization help the main idea stand out?

See the sample response, page 185.

Developing the Body

Revise this example:

> **A butterfly is hatched. From the eggs hatch larvae, or caterpillars. The egg is laid. The caterpillar turns into a chrysalis and hibernates.**

Develop the body by putting details in the right place to guide your reader. Apply all your organization skills, including using sequence words.

_____

_____

_____

_____

_____

_____

_____

_____

Think ABOUT

- Have I shown the reader where to slow down and where to speed up?

- Do all the details fit where they are placed?

- Will the reader find it easy to follow my ideas?

- Does the organization help the main idea stand out?

See the sample response, page 185.

 **Developing the Body**

Revise this example:

> **Put the cans in the red bin. Recycling helps the environment. Take the bins to the recycle center once a week. Separate the glass from the cans. New products can be made from recycled material. Put the glass in the blue bin.**

Develop the body by putting details in the right place to guide your reader. Apply all your organization skills, including using sequence words.

_____

_____

_____

_____

_____

_____

Think ABOUT

- Have I shown the reader where to slow down and where to speed up?
- Do all the details fit where they are placed?
- Will the reader find it easy to follow my ideas?
- Does the organization help the main idea stand out?

See the sample response, page 185.

Developing the Body

1. Read this example. Cross out any sentences that don't belong:

I was having the worst day ever. First I brushed my teeth. My dentist is Dr. Lavoie. I rode on the bus and it was really late. I had to wait and wait for the bus. When it came, there was hardly any room for me and my backpack. My backpack is getting really old and needs to be replaced. I haven't cleaned it out in ages. I think there is an old apple at the bottom of it. When I got to school I had missed my favorite class. I wonder when we'll have lunch.

2. Revise it on a separate sheet of paper, using the Think About questions to delete any sentences that don't fit with the main idea and strengthen the ones that do.

Think ABOUT

- Have I shown the reader where to slow down and where to speed up?
- Do all the details fit where they are placed?
- Will the reader find it easy to follow my ideas?
- Does the organization help the main idea stand out?

3. Use the student-friendly scoring guide to score your writing:

1 2 3 4 5

See the sample response, page 185, and the student-friendly scoring guide, page 52.

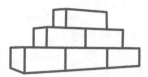

ORGANIZATION

Think ABOUT

ENDING WITH A SENSE OF RESOLUTION

- Have I wrapped up all the loose ends?

- Have I ended at the best place?

- Do I have an ending that makes my writing feel finished?

- Did I leave the reader with something to think about?

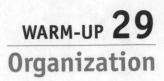

Ending With a Sense of Resolution

Revise one of these endings of a story about something mysterious that happened:

a. The end.
b. And that's all I remember about that day.
c. I hope you enjoyed my story.

End with a conclusion that wraps up your ideas and leaves your reader thinking.

_____

_____

_____

_____

_____

_____

_____

Think ABOUT

- Have I wrapped up all the loose ends?

- Have I ended at the best place?

- Do I have an ending that makes my writing feel finished?

- Did I leave the reader with something to think about?

See the sample response, page 185.

Ending With a Sense of Resolution

Revise this ending of a persuasive piece on voting age:

> **And now you know the three reasons why kids should be allowed to vote. That's all I have to say about that. So in conclusion, I hope you learned something from my paper.**

End with a conclusion that wraps up your ideas and leaves your reader thinking.

_____

_____

_____

_____

_____

_____

_____

_____

Think ABOUT

- Have I wrapped up all the loose ends?
- Have I ended at the best place?
- Do I have an ending that makes my writing feel finished?
- Did I leave the reader with something to think about?

See the sample response, page 186.

Ending With a Sense of Resolution

Revise this ending of an expository piece on tarantulas:

Thank you for reading my paper on tarantulas. That's all I have to say about tarantulas. Now you know a lot more about tarantulas.

End with a conclusion that wraps up your ideas and leaves your reader thinking.

_____

_____

_____

_____

_____

_____

_____

_____

Think ABOUT

- Have I wrapped up all the loose ends?
- Have I ended at the best place?
- Do I have an ending that makes my writing feel finished?
- Did I leave the reader with something to think about?

See the sample response, page 186.

Ending With a Sense of Resolution

1. Read the four endings and cross out any that do not work. Circle any that you think might be effective and revise them to fit the end of a "My Awful Monday" story.

   a. Those are all the reasons why my day was terrible.

   b. Can someone wave a magic wand and let me do last Monday over?

   c. Even my dog, Marco, seemed happy that the day was over.

   d. The end. I woke up and it was only a dream.

2. Write a draft of the story on a separate sheet of paper, using the Think About questions to ensure the piece ends with a sense of resolution.

> ## *Think* ABOUT
>
> - Have I wrapped up all the loose ends?
> - Have I ended at the best place?
> - Do I have an ending that makes my writing feel finished?
> - Did I leave the reader with something to think about?

3. Use the student-friendly scoring guide to score your writing:

   1 2 3 4 5

See the sample response, page 186, and the student-friendly scoring guide, page 52.

Organization

The Internal Structure of the Piece

I know where I'm going.

My opening will hook my reader!

The ending really works!

Ready to share!

5

Follow me!

I see just how all the parts fit together.

The middle makes sense, but it plods along.

My beginning is OK.

Halfway home!

4

My paper is PRETTY easy to follow.

Maybe I need to move some things around.

The ending doesn't grab me yet.

3

How do I begin?

This is confusing.

What should I tell first?

What comes next?

Help! Which pieces go together?

I don't know where I'm headed.

How do I end this?

Just beginning

2

1

VOICE

Think ABOUT

ESTABLISHING A TONE

- Can I name the primary voice of my writing? (For example, happy, frustrated, knowledgeable, scared, convincing)

- Have I varied the tone from the beginning to the end?

- Have I been expressive?

- Did I show that I care about this topic?

 **Establishing a Tone**

Revise this example:

It was my first time bungee jumping. I was excited. I was a little scared, but I knew I'd like it once I went.

Establish a tone that adds energy and makes your reader feel a certain way.

_____

_____

_____

_____

_____

_____

_____

_____

Think ABOUT

- Can I name the primary voice of my writing? (For example, happy, frustrated, knowledgeable, scared, convincing)

- Have I varied the tone from the beginning to the end?

- Have I been expressive?

- Did I show that I care about this topic?

See the sample response, page 186.

 **Establishing a Tone**

Revise this example:

Abraham Lincoln was born in 1809. He was a great president. He helped to free the slaves during the Civil War. He believed that the country could overcome any problems.

Establish a tone that adds energy and makes your reader feel a certain way.

_____

_____

_____

_____

_____

_____

_____

_____

Think ABOUT

- Can I name the primary voice of my writing? (For example, happy, frustrated, knowledgeable, scared, convincing)
- Have I varied the tone from the beginning to the end?
- Have I been expressive?
- Did I show that I care about this topic?

See the sample response, page 186.

 **Establishing a Tone**

Revise this example:

Young people should be aware of what goes on in politics. One day you will be able to vote, and it will be important to know who to support. You might even want to run for office yourself.

Establish a tone that adds energy and makes your reader feel a certain way.

_____

_____

_____

_____

_____

_____

_____

_____

Think ABOUT

- Can I name the primary voice of my writing? (For example, happy, frustrated, knowledgeable, scared, convincing)
- Have I varied the tone from the beginning to the end?
- Have I been expressive?
- Did I show that I care about this topic?

See the sample response, page 186.

 **Establishing a Tone**

1. Read this example:

My backpack is too large for me, and I put too much in it. I have a hard time carrying my backpack because it's so heavy. My shoulders hurt. Next year I'm going to get a smaller backpack. My shoulders won't hurt as much. I'll have to be more organized.

2. Revise it on a separate sheet of paper, using the Think About questions to select a voice that works well. Add details to make the voice stronger and more energetic.

Think ABOUT

- Can I name the primary voice of my writing? (For example, happy, frustrated, knowledgeable, scared, convincing)

- Have I varied the tone from the beginning to the end?

- Have I been expressive?

- Did I show that I care about this topic?

3. Use the student-friendly scoring guide to score your writing:

1 2 3 4 5

See the sample response, page 186, and the student-friendly scoring guide, page 73.

VOICE

Think ABOUT

CONVEYING THE PURPOSE

- Is the purpose of my writing clear?

- Does my point of view come through?

- Is this the right tone for this kind of writing?

- Have I used strong voice throughout this piece?

 **Conveying the Purpose**

Revise one of these examples:

a. I remember the day I got my first bike. (narrative: to tell a story)

b. Bicycle riders should follow the same rules of the road as cars.
(persuasive: to construct an argument)

c. To maintain a bike, there are only a few simple things to learn.
(expository: to inform or explain)

Let your voice convey and reinforce the purpose of your piece.

_____

_____

_____

_____

_____

_____

Think ABOUT

- Is the purpose of my writing clear?

- Does my point of view come through?

- Is this the right tone for this kind of writing?

- Have I used strong voice throughout this piece?

See the sample response, page 186.

 **Conveying the Purpose**

Revise one of these examples:

    a. Frogs are fascinating amphibians. (expository)

    b. Frogs should not be dissected in science class because it is cruel.
      (persuasive)

    c. Robert dared Julio to drop the frog down the shirt of the new kid.
      (narrative)

Let your voice convey and reinforce the purpose of your piece.

_____

_____

_____

_____

_____

_____

_____

Think ABOUT

- Is the purpose of my writing clear?

- Does my point of view come through?

- Is this the right tone for this kind of writing?

- Have I used strong voice throughout this piece?

See the sample response, page 186.

Conveying the Purpose

Revise one of these examples:

    a. I'll never forget my first day in Mr. Boudreau's class. (narrative)

    b. Although Mr. Boudreau is strict and has high standards, I think he is one of the best teachers at our school. (persuasive)

    c. Mr. Boudreau has all the qualities of a really great teacher. (expository)

Let your voice convey and reinforce the purpose of your piece.

_____

_____

_____

_____

_____

_____

_____

Think ABOUT

- Is the purpose of my writing clear?

- Does my point of view come through?

- Is this the right tone for this kind of writing?

- Have I used strong voice throughout this piece?

See the sample response, page 187.

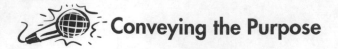 **Conveying the Purpose**

1. Read this example, listening for its voice:

Kids these days have it rough. Their backpacks are so heavy that they can hardly lift them. They have so much homework that they can never get it all done. Teachers need to stop assigning homework and then students won't have so many heavy books in their backpacks. It's all the teachers' fault.

2. What voice do you hear? Revise the piece on a separate sheet of paper, using the Think About questions to help you write in a more appropriate voice.

Think ABOUT

- Is the purpose of my writing clear?
- Does my point of view come through?
- Is this the right tone for this kind of writing?
- Have I used strong voice throughout this piece?

3. Use the student-friendly scoring guide to score your writing:

1 2 3 4 5

See the sample response, page 187, and the student-friendly scoring guide, page 73.

VOICE

Think ABOUT

CREATING A CONNECTION TO THE AUDIENCE

- Have I thought about the reader?

- Is this the right voice for this audience?

- Have I shown what matters most to me in this piece?

- Will the reader know how I think and feel?

Creating a Connection to the Audience

Revise this example:

The golden retriever is my favorite kind of dog. They are nice and loyal dogs. I had one when I was younger.

Choose an audience and then connect to that audience by giving important, appropriate details.

_____

_____

_____

_____

_____

_____

_____

_____

Think ABOUT

- Have I thought about the reader?
- Is this the right voice for this audience?
- Have I shown what matters most to me in this piece?
- Will the reader know how I think and feel?

See the sample response, page 187.

Creating a Connection to the Audience

Revise one of these examples:

a. **To an employer: "Hey, Dude. Gonna tell ya why I was late; I was totally wiped out, man."**

b. **To a friend: "Perhaps you might care to use the telephone and call me at the appointed hour that you find most convenient."**

c. **To a police officer: "I just did an ollie and slappy. What's the big deal? It's not like I slammed or nothing."**

Choose an audience and then connect to that audience by giving important, appropriate details.

_____

_____

_____

_____

_____

Think ABOUT

- Have I thought about the reader?
- Is this the right voice for this audience?
- Have I shown what matters most to me in this piece?
- Will the reader know how I think and feel?

See the sample response, page 187.

Creating a Connection to the Audience

Revise this example:

Dear Principal,

I think the rule about not wearing hats is stupid. Who made that ridiculous rule, anyway? It's not fair. If kids want to wear hats, it should be up to them. You should change this dumb rule and do it today, dude.

From: A Hat-Loving Student

Connect to the principal by giving important, appropriate details.

_____

_____

_____

_____

_____

_____

Think ABOUT

- Have I thought about the reader?
- Is this the right voice for this audience?
- Have I shown what matters most to me in this piece?
- Will the reader know how I think and feel?

See the sample response, page 187.

Creating a Connection to the Audience

1. Read this example:

> **Blue backpacks are my favorite. But I like black, too. Mostly I like backpacks that have a lot of pockets and zippers. I like to store my favorite things in my backpack so that when I get bored, I can pull them out to play when I have a spare minute or two. Some backpacks have thick shoulder pads. Some don't. It's important to me to get exactly the right one.**

2. Choose an audience and revise the piece on a separate sheet of paper, using the Think About questions to help you show what the reader needs to know.

Think ABOUT

- Have I thought about the reader?

- Is this the right voice for this audience?

- Have I shown what matters most to me in this piece?

- Will the reader know how I think and feel?

3. Use the student-friendly scoring guide to score your writing:

1 2 3 4 5

See the sample response, page 187, and the student-friendly scoring guide, page 73.

VOICE

Think ABOUT

TAKING RISKS TO CREATE VOICE

- Have I used words that are not ordinary?

- Is my writing interesting, fresh, and original?

- Have I tried to make my writing sound like me?

- Have I tried something different than what I've done before?

 **Taking Risks to Create Voice**

Revise this example:

> **It was a fun Fourth of July. We shot off fireworks and ate dessert at my friend Jesse's house before it was time to go home.**

Use words to create voice and bring the piece to life.

_____

_____

_____

_____

_____

_____

_____

_____

Think ABOUT

- Have I used words that are not ordinary?
- Is my writing interesting, fresh, and original?
- Have I tried to make my writing sound like me?
- Have I tried something different than what I've done before?

See the sample response, page 187.

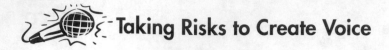 **Taking Risks to Create Voice**

Revise this example:

My home state is _____. I've lived there all my life. We have a unique way of living and talking in my state.

Use words to create voice and bring the piece to life.

_____

_____

_____

_____

_____

_____

_____

_____

_____

Think ABOUT

- Have I used words that are not ordinary?

- Is my writing interesting, fresh, and original?

- Have I tried to make my writing sound like me?

- Have I tried something different than what I've done before?

See the sample response, page 187.

 **Taking Risks to Create Voice**

Revise this example:

Last night I played my best game of basketball ever. It was very fun. I played the whole game. My team won.

Use words to create voice and bring the piece to life.

_____

_____

_____

_____

_____

_____

_____

_____

Think ABOUT

- Have I used words that are not ordinary?
- Is my writing interesting, fresh, and original?
- Have I tried to make my writing sound like me?
- Have I tried something different than what I've done before?

See the sample response, page 188.

Taking Risks to Create Voice

1. Read this example of a piece with *strong* voice:

> **Dear Teacher,**
>
> **Please don't load me up like an elephant on a safari—I'm not such a big creature! I admit, I need to be the one to clean my backpack out and get rid of the trash (like that old rotting apple), but you can also help by keeping the homework reasonable. So, let's think about this as a win-win situation. I'll keep my backpack spotlessly clean (and smelling fine) if you don't assign homework from more than one or two books a night.**
>
> **Sincerely,**

2. Revise it on a separate sheet of paper, *taking out* the voice to make the piece bland, uninteresting, and lacking energy.

Think ABOUT

- Have I used words that are not ordinary?
- Is my writing interesting, fresh, and original?
- Have I tried to make my writing sound like me?
- Have I done something different than what I've tried before?

3. Use the student-friendly scoring guide to score your writing:

1 2 3 4 5

See sample response, page 188, and student-friendly scoring guide, page 73.

Voice

The Tone of the Piece— the Personal Stamp of the Writer

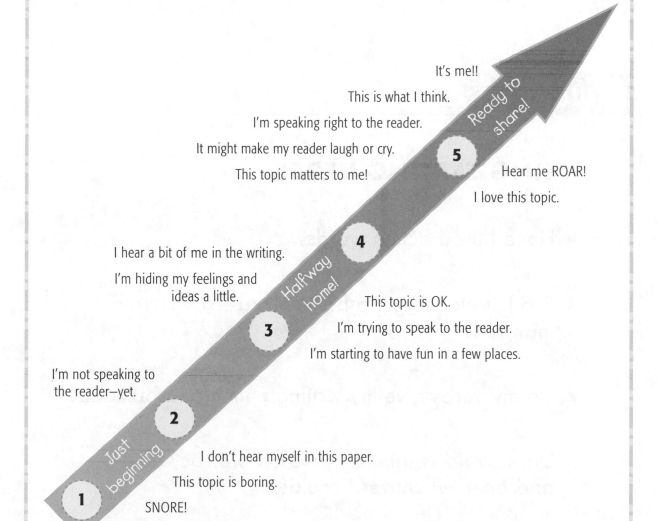

It's me!!

This is what I think.

I'm speaking right to the reader.

It might make my reader laugh or cry.

This topic matters to me!

Ready to share!

5

Hear me ROAR!

I love this topic.

I hear a bit of me in the writing.

I'm hiding my feelings and ideas a little.

Halfway home!

4

This topic is OK.

I'm trying to speak to the reader.

I'm starting to have fun in a few places.

3

I'm not speaking to the reader—yet.

2

Just beginning

I don't hear myself in this paper.

This topic is boring.

1

SNORE!

I wish I didn't have to do this.

WORD CHOICE

Think ABOUT

USING STRONG VERBS

- Have I used action words?

- Did I stretch to get a better word—*scurry* rather than *run*?

- Do my verbs give my writing punch and pizzazz?

- Did I avoid *is, am, are, was, were, be, being,* and *been* whenever I could?

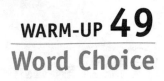

 **Using Strong Verbs**

Revise this example:

I am going to see my grandmother. It is going to be fun to go on the train and be with her. She tells good stories.

Select verbs that will strengthen your writing.

_____

_____

_____

_____

_____

_____

_____

_____

Think ABOUT

- Have I used action words?

- Did I stretch to get a better word—*scurry* rather than *run*?

- Do my verbs give my writing punch and pizzazz?

- Did I avoid *is, am, are, was, were, be, being,* and *been* whenever I could?

See the sample response, page 188.

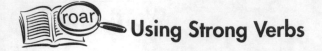
Using Strong Verbs

Revise this example:

Fire ants are pests. They are dangerous, too. If you get bitten by one, it can hurt a lot.

Select verbs that will strengthen your writing.

_____

_____

_____

_____

_____

_____

_____

_____

_____

Think ABOUT

- Have I used action words?

- Did I stretch to get a better word—*scurry* rather than *run*?

- Do my verbs give my writing punch and pizzazz?

- Did I avoid *is, am, are, was, were, be, being,* and *been* whenever I could?

See the sample response, page 188.

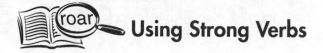 **Using Strong Verbs**

Revise this example:

The tornado was very close to my house. It was windy and loud. It made me nervous. I was scared.

Select verbs that will strengthen your writing.

_____

_____

_____

_____

_____

_____

_____

_____

Think ABOUT

- Have I used action words?

- Did I stretch to get a better word—*scurry* rather than *run*?

- Do my verbs give my writing punch and pizzazz?

- Did I avoid *is, am, are, was, were, be, being,* and *been* whenever I could?

See the sample response, page 188.

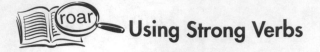
Using Strong Verbs

1. Read this example and circle the verbs:

> I like bananas. But not when they are green. That means they are not ripe. When they are ripe, they are soft. I like them that way. You can eat them ripe or not ripe. Either way they are good for you to eat. Bananas are a very healthy food. They have potassium. They are in different colors: red, yellow, and green.

2. Revise it on a separate sheet of paper, using the Think About questions to help you add stronger verbs that energize the writing and make it more interesting to read.

Think ABOUT

- Have I used action words?
- Did I stretch to get a better word—*scurry* rather than *run*?
- Do my verbs give my writing punch and pizzazz?
- Did I avoid *is, am, are, was, were, be, being,* and *been* whenever I could?

3. Use the student-friendly scoring guide to score your writing:

1 2 3 4 5

See the sample response, page 188, and the student-friendly scoring guide, page 94.

WORD CHOICE

KEY QUALITIES

Using Strong Verbs

Using Striking Words and Phrases

Using Words That Are Specific and Accurate

Using Language Effectively

Think ABOUT

USING STRIKING WORDS AND PHRASES

- Did I try to use words that sound "just right"?

- Did I try hyphenating several shorter words to make an interesting-sounding new word?

- Did I try putting words with the same sound together?

- Did I read my piece aloud to find at least one or two moments that I love?

roar — **Using Striking Words and Phrases**

Revise this example:

It was a dark and stormy night. The wind was blowing. It felt like it might rain.

Use striking words and phrases to make the writing sound more interesting.

_____

_____

_____

_____

_____

_____

_____

_____

Think ABOUT

- Did I try to use words that sound "just right"?

- Did I try hyphenating several shorter words to make an interesting-sounding new word?

- Did I try putting words with the same sound together?

- Did I read my piece aloud to find at least one or two moments that I love?

See the sample response, page 188.

 **Using Striking Words and Phrases**

Revise this example:

> **People are concerned about the Earth getting too hot. If what people say is true, our planet's temperature could change a lot over the next few years.**

Use striking words and phrases to make the writing sound more interesting.

_____

_____

_____

_____

_____

_____

_____

Think ABOUT

- Did I try to use words that sound "just right"?

- Did I try hyphenating several shorter words to make an interesting-sounding new word?

- Did I try putting words with the same sound together?

- Did I read my piece aloud to find at least one or two moments that I love?

See the sample response, page 188.

roar **Using Striking Words and Phrases**

Revise this example:

The food at school isn't very good. It's pretty bad, actually. It doesn't have much taste, and it's boring to eat the same thing day after day. I don't care for the food at school. I'd rather bring my own lunch.

Use striking words and phrases to make the writing sound more interesting.

_____

_____

_____

_____

_____

_____

_____

Think ABOUT

- Did I try to use words that sound "just right"?

- Did I try hyphenating several shorter words to make an interesting-sounding new word?

- Did I try putting words with the same sound together?

- Did I read my piece aloud to find at least one or two moments that I love?

See the sample response, page 188.

Using Striking Words and Phrases

1. Read this example:

My little brother makes a bad sound when he eats bananas. I think it is bad that he chews with his mouth open, because you can see the bananas. No matter how much I tell him not to, he does it anyway.

2. Revise it on a separate sheet of paper, using the Think About questions to help you choose words that let the reader share your experience and emotions.

Think ABOUT

- Did I try to use words that sound "just right"?
- Did I try hyphenating several shorter words to make an interesting-sounding new word?
- Did I try putting words with the same sound together?
- Did I read my piece aloud to find at least one or two moments that I love?

3. Use the student-friendly scoring guide to score your writing:

1 2 3 4 5

See the sample response, page 188, and the student-friendly scoring guide, page 94.

WORD CHOICE

Think ABOUT

USING WORDS THAT ARE SPECIFIC AND ACCURATE

- Have I used nouns and modifiers that help the reader see a picture?

- Did I avoid using words that might confuse the reader?

- If I tried a new word, did I check to make sure I used it correctly?

- Are these the best words that can be used?

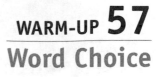

 **Using Words That Are Specific and Accurate**

Revise this example:

> **There are many different butterflies. Some are sorta big, while others are much smaller. Some butterflies fly a long way every year.**

Use specific and accurate words to show your reader exactly what you're talking about. (You may want to check an encyclopedia or appropriate Web site for words.)

_____

_____

_____

_____

_____

_____

_____

Think ABOUT

- Have I used nouns and modifiers that help the reader see a picture?

- Did I avoid using words that might confuse the reader?

- If I tried a new word, did I check to make sure I used it correctly?

- Are these the best words that can be used?

See the sample response, page 188.

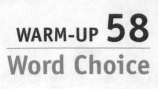 **Using Words That Are Specific and Accurate**

Revise this example:

My brother is a beginning surfer. He can't even do basic tricks yet, so forget about the hard ones. He'll always stay a beginner unless he learns how to surf.

Use specific and accurate words to show your reader exactly what you're talking about. (You may want to check an encyclopedia or appropriate Web site for words.)

_____

_____

_____

_____

_____

_____

_____

Think ABOUT

- Have I used nouns and modifiers that help the reader see a picture?

- Did I avoid using words that might confuse the reader?

- If I tried a new word, did I check to make sure I used it correctly?

- Are these the best words that can be used?

See the sample response, page 188.

 **Using Words That Are Specific and Accurate**

Revise this example:

My best friend is so nice. She's funny. She's really funny when we go to the mall and hang out together. We like to do fun things that make us laugh a lot. When we go out to eat we always order good things.

Use specific and accurate words to show your reader exactly what you're talking about. (You may want to check an encyclopedia or appropriate Web site for words.)

_____

_____

_____

_____

_____

_____

Think ABOUT

- Have I used nouns and modifiers that help the reader see a picture?

- Did I avoid using words that might confuse the reader?

- If I tried a new word, did I check to make sure I used it correctly?

- Are these the best words that can be used?

See the sample response, page 189.

roar **Using Words That Are Specific and Accurate**

1. Read this example. Underline words that could be replaced:

Bananas are sort of good for you to eat. They have lots of healthy stuff in them. Sometimes they can be good for your heart, your skin, and for not getting stressed out.

2. Revise it on a separate sheet of paper, using the Think About questions to choose words that are clear and specific and add helpful information for the reader.

> ## *Think* ABOUT
>
> - Have I used nouns and modifiers that help the reader see a picture?
> - Did I avoid using words that might confuse the reader?
> - If I tried a new word, did I check to make sure I used it correctly?
> - Are these the best words that can be used?

3. Use the student-friendly scoring guide to score your writing:

1 2 3 4 5

See the sample response, page 189, and the student-friendly scoring guide, page 94.

WORD CHOICE

Think ABOUT

USING LANGUAGE EFFECTIVELY

- Did I choose words that show I really thought about them?

- Have I tried to use words without repeating myself?

- Do my words capture the reader's imagination?

- Have I found the best way to express myself?

roar **Using Language Effectively**

Revise this example:

I like my locker partner. She's great. She does nice things for me, and I appreciate it.

Use words that show how to use language effectively.

_____

_____

_____

_____

_____

_____

_____

_____

_____

Think ABOUT

- Did I choose words that show I really thought about them?

- Have I tried to use words without repeating myself?

- Do my words capture the reader's imagination?

- Have I found the best way to express myself?

See the sample response, page 189.

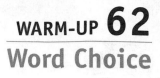

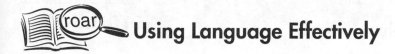 **Using Language Effectively**

Revise this example:

Every day, lions and their mates must hunt for food. If lions didn't hunt for food, they would starve. Mostly the female lion hunts, and the male lion waits for her to bring back the food for him and the cubs.

Use words that show how to use language effectively.

_____

_____

_____

_____

_____

_____

_____

Think ABOUT

- Did I choose words that show I really thought about them?
- Have I tried to use words without repeating myself?
- Do my words capture the reader's imagination?
- Have I found the best way to express myself?

See the sample response, page 189.

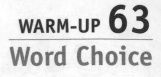

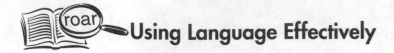**Using Language Effectively**

Revise this example:

I went to the art museum. I saw lots of paintings and sculptures. The paintings and sculptures were interesting to see. I'm glad I went to the art museum because the paintings and sculptures were nice.

Use words that show how to use language effectively.

_____

_____

_____

_____

_____

_____

_____

Think ABOUT

- Did I choose words that show I really thought about them?
- Have I tried to use words without repeating myself?
- Do my words capture the reader's imagination?
- Have I found the best way to express myself?

See the sample response, page 189.

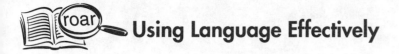 **Using Language Effectively**

1. Read this example. Circle any words that are not clear or are used inappropriately:

Bananas are a fine food for humans. I consume bananas on a daily basis. Bananas are a decent and pleasurable fruit to consume, even if you only need an additional food source in the middle of the day. One should consider the inclusion of bananas to one's dietary supplemental scheme.

2. Revise it on a separate sheet of paper, using the Think About questions to choose words that sound more natural and capture the way you speak.

> ### *Think* ABOUT
>
> - Did I choose words that show I really thought about them?
> - Have I tried to use words without repeating myself?
> - Do my words capture the reader's imagination?
> - Have I found the best way to express myself?

3. Use the student-friendly scoring guide to score your writing:

1 2 3 4 5

See the sample response, page 189, and the student-friendly scoring guide, page 94.

Word Choice

The Vocabulary the Writer Uses to Convey Meaning

My words paint a picture.

My words make the message CLEAR.

I like the way my words sound and feel.

Ready to share!

5

I think this is the BEST way to say it!

I need more IMAGINATION here!

Some of the words and phrases are great, but some need work.

Some words are really vague.

4

Halfway home!

These are some of the first words I thought of.

3

There is probably a BETTER way to say it, but this is my first try.

2

Just beginning

These words are NOT my favorites.

The words I've used don't paint a picture in the reader's mind.

Some of my words don't make sense to me when I read them over.

1

These words just don't make sense.

SENTENCE FLUENCY

KEY QUALITIES

Crafting Well-Built Sentences

Varying Sentence Patterns

Breaking the "Rules" to Create Fluency

Capturing a Smooth and Rhythmic Flow

Think ABOUT

CRAFTING WELL-BUILT SENTENCES

- Do my sentences begin in different ways?

- Are my sentences different lengths?

- Are my sentences built with sturdy construction?

- Have I used transitions (*but, and, so*) to connect parts of sentences?

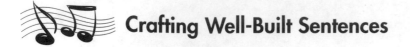 **Crafting Well-Built Sentences**

Revise this example:

I lost two more teeth. I lost my two pointy front teeth. They came out the same day. They were wiggly for two days.

Craft well-built sentences to create a paragraph that flows.

_____

_____

_____

_____

_____

_____

_____

_____

_____

Think ABOUT

- Do my sentences begin in different ways?

- Are my sentences different lengths?

- Are my sentences built with sturdy construction?

- Have I used transitions (*but, and, so*) to connect parts of sentences?

See the sample response, page 189.

Crafting Well-Built Sentences

Revise this example:

Exercise is good for you. Exercise gives you energy. Exercise is a way to work off stress. Exercise can make your body stronger. Everyone should exercise.

Craft well-built sentences to create a paragraph that flows.

_____

_____

_____

_____

_____

_____

_____

_____

Think ABOUT

- Do my sentences begin in different ways?

- Are my sentences different lengths?

- Are my sentences built with sturdy construction?

- Have I used transitions (*but, and, so*) to connect parts of sentences?

See the sample response, page 189.

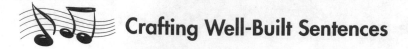
Crafting Well-Built Sentences

Revise this example:

**I have the flu. I feel terrible. I can't sleep. I'm restless. I'm grouchy.
I'm not a good patient. I wish I could rest. I hate the flu.**

Craft well-built sentences to create a paragraph that flows.

_____

_____

_____

_____

_____

_____

_____

_____

Think ABOUT

- Do my sentences begin in different ways?

- Are my sentences different lengths?

- Are my sentences built with sturdy construction?

- Have I used transitions (*but, and, so*) to connect parts of sentences?

See the sample response, page 189.

Crafting Well-Built Sentences

1. Read this example:

> **Soccer is the best sport you can play. Soccer is exciting. Soccer is a lot of fun. Soccer is a game you can play when you are little. Soccer is a game you can play when you get older, too. Soccer is a lifelong sport. Soccer is a favorite game for people around the world.**

2. Revise it on a separate sheet of paper, using the Think About questions to create new sentences of different lengths that begin in different ways, so that they're more pleasing to the ear.

Think ABOUT

- Do my sentences begin in different ways?

- Are my sentences different lengths?

- Are my sentences built with sturdy construction?

- Have I used transitions (*but, and, so*) to connect parts of sentences?

3. Use the student-friendly scoring guide to score your writing:

1 2 3 4 5

See the sample response, page 190, and the student-friendly scoring guide, page 115.

SENTENCE FLUENCY

Think ABOUT

VARYING SENTENCE PATTERNS

- Did I use different kinds of sentences?

- Did I make some of my sentences complex?

- Did I make some of my sentences simple?

- Did I vary my sentence types from one to the next?

 **Varying Sentence Patterns**

Revise this example:

Family vacations are really boring. My family never does anything fun. We always go to the same places. We always do the same things. I want to do something different.

Vary the sentence patterns in your new paragraph.

_____

_____

_____

_____

_____

_____

_____

_____

Think ABOUT

- Did I use different kinds of sentences?

- Did I make some of my sentences complex?

- Did I make some of my sentences simple?

- Did I vary my sentence types from one to the next?

See the sample response, page 190.

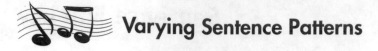 **Varying Sentence Patterns**

Revise this example:

Rainy days can be fun. There are many fun things to do on a rainy day. On a rainy day you could write a play. You could make costumes and act out the play.

Vary the sentence patterns in your new paragraph.

_____

_____

_____

_____

_____

_____

_____

_____

Think ABOUT

- Did I use different kinds of sentences?
- Did I make some of my sentences complex?
- Did I make some of my sentences simple?
- Did I vary my sentence types from one to the next?

See the sample response, page 190.

 **Varying Sentence Patterns**

Revise this example:

I play the trombone in the school band. I like to play the trombone because it makes a great sound. I jumped at the chance to play trombone. I have enjoyed it since the first day I started.

Vary the sentence patterns in your new paragraph.

_____

_____

_____

_____

_____

_____

_____

_____

Think ABOUT

- Did I use different kinds of sentences?
- Did I make some of my sentences complex?
- Did I make some of my sentences simple?
- Did I vary my sentence types from one to the next?

See the sample response, page 190.

Varying Sentence Patterns

1. Read this example:

> **Learning to head butt is hard. It's an important soccer skill. You will have to practice.**

2. Revise it on a separate sheet of paper, using the Think About questions to help you write sentences of different types—both short and simple and long and complex.

Think ABOUT

- Did I use different kinds of sentences?
- Did I make some of my sentences complex?
- Did I make some of my sentences simple?
- Did I vary my sentence types from one to the next?

3. Use the student-friendly scoring guide to score your writing:

1 2 3 4 5

See the sample response, page 190, and the student-friendly scoring guide, page 115.

SENTENCE FLUENCY

Think ABOUT

BREAKING THE "RULES" TO CREATE FLUENCY

- Do my fragments add style?

- Did I begin a sentence informally to make it conversational?

- Did I make dialogue sound real?

- Did I try a one-word sentence to add emphasis?

Breaking the "Rules" to Create Fluency

Revise this example:

When you walk in the woods with my friend Tim, he makes a lot of noise. When you walk with him, he steps on twigs and big branches. He runs into everything out in the woods, and it all makes noise. He walks with heavy feet. He scares the animals away.

Try something different and break some sentence "rules" to make your piece fluent.

_____

_____

_____

_____

_____

_____

_____

Think ABOUT

- Do my fragments add style?
- Did I begin a sentence informally to make it conversational?
- Did I make dialogue sound real?
- Did I try a one-word sentence to add emphasis?

See the sample response, page 190.

Breaking the "Rules" to Create Fluency

Revise this example:

Buying the right kind of athletic shoes is important. To be sure, buying athletic shoes that are comfortable is one thing you should consider. Buying athletic shoes that are sturdy is another important consideration. Buying athletic shoes that you like is important, too, but not as important as comfort and durability.

Try something different and break some sentence "rules" to make your piece fluent.

_____

_____

_____

_____

_____

_____

_____

Think ABOUT

- Do my fragments add style?
- Did I begin a sentence informally to make it conversational?
- Did I make dialogue sound real?
- Did I try a one-word sentence to add emphasis?

See the sample response, page 190.

Breaking the "Rules" to Create Fluency

Revise this example:

When I was little, I was afraid of the dark. I used to hide in my closet at night and listen for the night noises. I didn't know the sound that pipes make. I also didn't know how windows sound in the wind. I hid in my closet waiting for morning many nights.

Try something different and break some sentence "rules" to make your piece fluent.

_____

_____

_____

_____

_____

_____

_____

Think ABOUT

- Do my fragments add style?
- Did I begin a sentence informally to make it conversational?
- Did I make dialogue sound real?
- Did I try a one-word sentence to add emphasis?

See the sample response, page 190.

Breaking the "Rules" to Create Fluency

1. Read this example:

> **My soccer coach yells at me during practice to run faster and harder. I try, but my heart beats fast when I run fast. My lungs have a hard time getting air when I run fast. My hard work is paying off though. We are now winning games on my soccer team. I say, "We've won three games since we've started practicing more." We're really excited to win more games.**

2. Revise it on a separate sheet of paper, using the Think About questions to make the sentences more fluent. Read your piece aloud to check for fluency.

Think ABOUT

- Do my fragments add style?
- Did I begin a sentence informally to make it conversational?
- Did I make dialogue sound real?
- Did I try a one-word sentence to add emphasis?

3. Use the student-friendly scoring guide to score your writing:

1 2 3 4 5

See the sample response, page 191, and the student-friendly scoring guide, page 115.

SENTENCE FLUENCY

Think ABOUT

CAPTURING A SMOOTH AND RHYTHMIC FLOW

- Is it easy to read my entire piece aloud?

- Do my sentences flow easily from one to the next?

- Do I have phrases that sound smooth when I read them aloud?

- Do my sentences have a pleasing tempo?

Capturing a Smooth and Rhythmic Flow

Revise this example:

My cat purrs softly. My cat likes to rub up next to me. My cat licks my hand. My cat is soft and cuddly.

Use smooth and rhythmic phrasing to make your sentences flow.

_____

_____

_____

_____

_____

_____

_____

_____

Think ABOUT

- Is it easy to read my entire piece aloud?

- Do my sentences flow easily from one to the next?

- Do I have phrases that sound smooth when I read them aloud?

- Do my sentences have a pleasing tempo?

See the sample response, page 191.

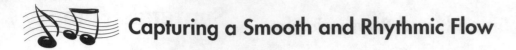 **Capturing a Smooth and Rhythmic Flow**

Revise this example:

Doing chores is boring. I hate taking out the trash. I hate cleaning my room. I hate doing the dishes. I wish I didn't have to do chores.

Use smooth and rhythmic phrasing to make your sentences flow.

_____

_____

_____

_____

_____

_____

_____

_____

Think ABOUT

- Is it easy to read my entire piece aloud?

- Do my sentences flow easily from one to the next?

- Do I have phrases that sound smooth when I read them aloud?

- Do my sentences have a pleasing tempo?

See the sample response, page 191.

Capturing a Smooth and Rhythmic Flow

Revise this example:

Don't look at your feet when you dance. Don't worry about counting steps. Don't pull at your clothes. Don't think about getting sweaty palms. Don't walk on your partner's feet. Don't make any sudden moves. Try to enjoy yourself.

Use smooth and rhythmic phrasing to make your sentences flow.

_____

_____

_____

_____

_____

_____

_____

Think ABOUT

- Is it easy to read my entire piece aloud?

- Do my sentences flow easily from one to the next?

- Do I have phrases that sound smooth when I read them aloud?

- Do my sentences have a pleasing tempo?

See the sample response, page 191.

♪♫ **Capturing a Smooth and Rhythmic Flow**

1. Read aloud this example of a piece with *strong* sentence fluency:

> **Imagine you are at the championship soccer game for your school. You are the goalie. The ball is dropped onto the field, and SMACK, one of your opposing teammates snags the ball, passing it to another as they run down the field toward the goal—the goal where you are standing—the goal where the game will be won or lost. Your heart races and you can feel your legs begin to move toward the ball without your even thinking about it. You grab the ball as it is kicked into the goal. Whew! Another save for you!**

2. On a separate sheet of paper, revise it to be *boring*, with awkward phrases and simple sentences. Read your piece aloud. If it sounds terrible, you've developed an ear for fluency!

Think ABOUT

- Is it easy to read my piece aloud?

- Do my sentences flow easily from one to the next?

- Do I have phrases that sound smooth when I read them aloud?

- Do my sentences have a pleasing tempo?

3. Use the student-friendly scoring guide to score your writing:

1 2 3 4 5

See the sample response, page 191, and the student-friendly scoring guide, page 115.

Sentence Fluency

The Rhythm and Flow of Words and Phrases

My paper is EASY to read out loud.

Some sentences are LONG and STRETCHY—some are SHORT and SNAPPY.

I like the sound of this paper—it has rhythm!

Ready to share!

5

My sentences begin in several different ways.

A lot of my sentences begin the same way.

I wish my paper sounded a little smoother in places.

Halfway home!

4

There are lots of choppy little sentences, one after another.

My sentences are all about the same length.

3

It's PRETTY easy to read out loud if you take your time.

2

Just beginning

Help! Some of these sentences don't make sense.

My paper is HARD to read out loud—even for me!

I can't tell where a new sentence begins.

1

Every word is strung together in one endless sentence.

REVISION CHECKLIST

Directions: Choose a piece you're working on and use this list to make sure you've applied all the traits.

I've revised for:

☐ **Ideas:** I've selected one topic, focused it, and used specific details to describe it.

☐ **Organization:** I've written an attention-grabbing lead, organized my details in a logical way, and wrapped it all up in the conclusion.

☐ **Voice:** I've written in a way that sets the right tone for my piece, targets my audience, and sounds fresh and original.

☐ **Word Choice:** I've used strong verbs and other specific and accurate words that add sparkle to my writing.

☐ **Sentence Fluency:** I've used sentences with different lengths and patterns to add rhythm to my writing, and I've taken some risks and tried some new ways to write sentences.

Traits in my writing that still need attention and my plan for improving them:

☐ Ideas: _____

_____

☐ Organization: _____

_____

☐ Voice: _____

_____

☐ Word Choice: _____

_____

☐ Sentence Fluency: _____

_____

Editing Warm-Ups

Editing is the stage in the writing process where writers clean up the text and get it ready for the reader. They check, among other things, their spelling, punctuation, capitalization, and grammar and usage to create a final copy. It can be challenging for young writers to apply these conventions with accuracy and consistency. The warm-ups that follow are intended to give them practice, with an eye toward helping them become independent, confident editors.

Skilled application of conventions ensures writing that is not only "correct," but also meaningful and comprehensible. Punctuation, for example, can guide readers or befuddle them. Nonstandard grammar can make for more authentic dialogue. Students learn how to use conventions, beginning with simple skills, such as capitalizing proper nouns and the first word in a sentence, and moving on to more difficult skills, such as knowing the right words to capitalize in a title. And since the conventions trait is made up of four broad editing zones—spelling, punctuation, capitalization, and grammar and usage—this section contains plenty for them to learn, regardless of where they are on the developmental ladder.

The first section contains warm-ups on individual conventions to give students a solid handle on how to apply them. The second section contains warm-ups that require students to apply multiple conventions in a single piece, providing a more authentic writing experience. The result: Students learn about conventions efficiently and effectively—and how to edit for themselves.

Follow the directions at the top of each page. Consult the answers at the back of the book and compare them to your students' responses. Focus on what students know and are doing correctly as much as on what they still need to learn. Doing this will surely put them on the road to becoming capable and self-assured editors.

Photocopy for students to keep in their notebooks.

EDITOR'S MARKS

℘	Delete material.	The writing is ~~is~~ good.
(sp)	Correct spelling or spell it out.	We are learning ②traits this (weak).
∩	Close space.	To day is publishing day.
∧	Insert a letter, word, or phrase.	My teacher has books. wonderful
∧	Change a letter.	She is a great wrọter.
/#/	Add a space.	Don't forget agood introduction.
∿	Transpose letters or words.	She rẹad the piece with flair!
≡	Change to a capital letter.	We have j. k. Rowling to thank for Harry Potter's magic.
/	Change to a lowercase letter.	The "Proof is in the Pudding" was his favorite saying.
¶	Start a new paragraph.	"What day is it?" he inquired. "It's Christmas," returned Tiny Tim.
⊙	Add a period.	Use all the traits as you write ⊙

Working With Individual

CONVENTIONS

Spelling

Punctuation

Capitalization

Grammar and Usage

Think ABOUT

SPELLING

- Have I checked words with *ie* and *ei*? To make the long-e sound, follow the rule "*i* before *e*, except after *c*" (*piece* and *receive*). To make any other sound, write *ei* (*eight, weight, rein*).

- Have I checked words ending in *y* when a suffix is added? (*Enjoy* becomes *enjoys*, but *apply* becomes *applies*.)

- Have I checked words that require a doubled consonant when a suffix is added? (*drag* becomes *dragging* but *enter* becomes *entering*)

- Have I checked words ending in silent *e* when a suffix is added? (*love* becomes *loving* but also *lovely*)

Photocopy for students to keep in their notebooks.

Rules to Remember FOR SPELLING

- When deciding whether to use *ie* or *ei*, follow these rules:

  For words with the long-*e* sound, follow the rule "*i* before *e* except after *c*."
  Examples: *piece* and *receive*
  Exceptions: *either, neither,* and *seize*

  Use *ei* to spell other sounds, such as the long-*a* sound.
  Examples: *eight* and *weight*

- When adding a suffix to a word that ends in *y*, change the *y* to *i* if a consonant precedes the *y*.
  Example: *penny* becomes *penniless; apply* becomes *applies* and *applied*.
  Exception: words ending in *ing: apply* becomes *applying*.

- If a vowel precedes the *y*, keep the *y* and add the suffix.
  Example: *toy* becomes *toys*.

- Double the final consonant in a word when adding a suffix if
  (a) the word is one syllable and
  (b) the final consonant is preceded by a single vowel.
  Example: *run* becomes *running*
  or
  (a) the last syllable of the word is stressed and
  (b) the final consonant is preceded by a single vowel.
  Example: *infer* becomes *inferred*.

- Do not double the final consonant if the stress is on the first syllable and not the last.
  Example: *enter* becomes *entering*.

- Drop the final, silent *e* before you add a suffix beginning with a vowel.
  Examples: *convince* becomes *convincing* and *love* becomes *loving*.

- Keep the final, silent *e* in place when you add a suffix beginning with a consonant.
  Example: *love* becomes *lovely*.

Add other important spelling rules you want to remember here:

_____

_____

 **Spelling**

> **Check the spelling of words with *ie* and *ei*.**

See answers, page 192.

WARM-UP 81 *Mark the errors:*

I beleive the pie Ray and I ate was cherry rhubarb, but niether of us is sure.

Rewrite the sentence correctly: _____

_____

Apply the rule in a sentence of your own: _____

_____

WARM-UP 82 *Mark the errors:*

My nieghbor's concieted neice thought her cookies were better than mine.

Rewrite the sentence correctly: _____

_____

Apply the rule in a sentence of your own: _____

_____

WARM-UP 83 *Mark the errors:*

My best freind was so full, she took a breif run to get some releif.

Rewrite the sentence correctly: _____

_____

Apply the rule in a sentence of your own: _____

_____

WARM-UP 84 *Mark the errors:*

The wieght of the cake I carried was so burdensome that I had to iether sieze it with both hands or let it drop.

Rewrite the sentence correctly: _____

_____

Apply the rule in a sentence of your own: _____

_____

WARM-UP 85 *Mark the errors:*

To my releif, the casheir put a reciept in the bag for the donuts I bought.

Rewrite the sentence correctly: _____

_____

Apply the rule in a sentence of your own: _____

_____

 **Spelling**

> **Check the spelling of words ending in _y_ when a suffix is added.**

See answers, page 192.

WARM-UP 86   _Mark the errors:_

The map shows red lines, signifiing Canada's boundarys.

Rewrite the sentence correctly: _____

_____

Apply the rule in a sentence of your own: _____

_____

WARM-UP 87   _Mark the errors:_

Ordinaryly, U.S. citizens must present a passport to temporaryly stay in Canada.

Rewrite the sentence correctly: _____

_____

Apply the rule in a sentence of your own: _____

_____

WARM-UP 88   *Mark the errors:*

"Will customs take long?" Mom worryed. "Not more than an hour,"
I replyed.

Rewrite the sentence correctly: _____

_____

Apply the rule in a sentence of your own: _____

_____

WARM-UP 89   *Mark the errors:*

A passport stamp signifys that you have successfully met the expectations of
the Canadian immigration authoritys and may enter the country.

Rewrite the sentence correctly: _____

_____

Apply the rule in a sentence of your own: _____

_____

WARM-UP 90   *Mark the errors:*

I liked the orderlyness of the communitys I visited in Canada.

Rewrite the sentence correctly: _____

_____

Apply the rule in a sentence of your own: _____

_____

Spelling

> **Check the spelling of words that require a doubled consonant when a suffix is added.**

See answers, page 193.

WARM-UP 91 *Mark the errors:*

The athlete admited that he had stoped short of the finish line.

Rewrite the sentence correctly: _____

_____

Apply the rule in a sentence of your own: _____

_____

WARM-UP 92 *Mark the errors:*

The weter the track became, the more danger it posed for the runer.

Rewrite the sentence correctly: _____

_____

Apply the rule in a sentence of your own: _____

_____

WARM-UP 93   *Mark the errors:*

The runer felt robed of his chance to break the course record.

Rewrite the sentence correctly: _____

_____

Apply the rule in a sentence of your own: _____

_____

WARM-UP 94   *Mark the errors:*

He returnned to the gym in a foul mood, admiting his disappointment.

Rewrite the sentence correctly: _____

_____

Apply the rule in a sentence of your own: _____

_____

WARM-UP 95   *Mark the errors:*

The coach reminded him that rain occured often in the spring and he should not worry about controling it.

Rewrite the sentence correctly: _____

_____

Apply the rule in a sentence of your own: _____

_____

 **Spelling**

Check the spelling of words ending in silent *e* when a suffix is added.

See answers, page 193.

WARM-UP 96   *Mark the errors:*

I am hopful that my garden is becomeing lush and colorful.

Rewrite the sentence correctly: _____

_____

Apply the rule in a sentence of your own: _____

_____

WARM-UP 97   *Mark the errors:*

Prepareing soil makes me grimey, but I enjoy scrapeing dirt
into buckets.

Rewrite the sentence correctly: _____

_____

Apply the rule in a sentence of your own: _____

_____

WARM-UP 98   *Mark the errors:*

I find myself hopeing these slimey slugs will be eaten by birds.

Rewrite the sentence correctly: _____

_____

Apply the rule in a sentence of your own: _____

_____

WARM-UP 99   *Mark the errors:*

The largeest rock over there is becomeing a problem in this lovly garden.

Rewrite the sentence correctly: _____

_____

Apply the rule in a sentence of your own: _____

_____

WARM-UP 100   *Mark the errors:*

If my garden continus to grow this well, I would be wasteing my time doing anything other than learning how to be a fameous gardener.

Rewrite the sentence correctly: _____

_____

Apply the rule in a sentence of your own: _____

_____

Working With Individual

CONVENTIONS

Spelling

Punctuation

Capitalization

Grammar and Usage

Think ABOUT

PUNCTUATION

- Did I punctuate the end of every sentence?

- Did I use commas to separate words in a series?

- Did I use apostrophes to show possessives and contractions?

- Did I use quotation marks to show dialogue and direct quotations?

Photocopy for students to keep in their notebooks.

Rules to Remember FOR PUNCTUATION

- Use punctuation to show the ending of every sentence.
  Choose a period (.), an exclamation mark (!), or a question mark (?).

- Use commas to separate words in a series and before the word *and*
  at the end of that series.
  Example: *I banged my head, my knee, and my elbows while I was at the playground with my little sister.*

- Use an apostrophe to show the possessive form of a noun.
  Example: *Mary Sue's dishes*
  Exception: the word *its: The tree lost its leaves.*

- Put the possessive apostrophe after the final *s* if a plural noun ends
  in *s* already.
  Example: *Four of my classmates' parents planned a big surprise party for us.*

- Use an apostrophe to show where letters have been dropped in contractions.
  Example *do not* becomes *don't; it is* becomes *it's.*

- Use quotation marks around dialogue and directly quoted material.
  Note: Commas and periods always go inside the quotation marks.
  Examples:
  "Oh no! I forgot my homework folder on the bus," said Jaycee.
  Jaycee said, "Oh no! I forgot my homework folder on the bus."
  "Oh no!" said Jaycee. "I forgot my homework folder on the bus."
  One movie review said, "This is simply the best children's movie of all time."

Add other important punctuation rules you want to remember here:

_____

_____

_____

_____

Punctuation

> **Punctuate the end of every sentence.**

See answers, page 194.

WARM-UP 101 *Mark the errors:*

The space shuttle is the most complex machine ever made

Rewrite the sentence correctly: _____

_____

Apply the rule in a sentence of your own: _____

_____

WARM-UP 102 *Mark the errors:*

Who would have imagined that space shuttle astronauts would work on the International Space Station as it orbits around the Earth

Rewrite the sentence correctly: _____

_____

Apply the rule in a sentence of your own: _____

_____

WARM-UP 103   *Mark the errors:*

How thrilling to see the Earth gradually growing smaller on the horizon

Rewrite the sentence correctly: _____

_____

Apply the rule in a sentence of your own: _____

_____

WARM-UP 104   *Mark the errors:*

"I want to become an astronaut," Franklin announced to his parents

Rewrite the sentence correctly: _____

_____

Apply the rule in a sentence of your own: _____

_____

WARM-UP 105   *Mark the errors:*

Wow Imagine how exciting it would be to float weightless in space

Rewrite the sentence correctly: _____

_____

Apply the rule in a sentence of your own: _____

_____

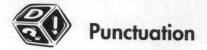

Punctuation

> **Use commas to separate words in a series.**

See answers, page 194.

WARM-UP 106 *Mark the errors:*

When I go to the movies, I always get popcorn candy and a soda.

Rewrite the sentence correctly: _____

_____

Apply the rule in a sentence of your own: _____

_____

WARM-UP 107 *Mark the errors:*

My favorite kind of pizza has olives artichokes sausage and extra cheese on top.

Rewrite the sentence correctly: _____

_____

Apply the rule in a sentence of your own: _____

_____

WARM-UP 108   *Mark the errors:*

After school I have to walk the dog take out the trash and do my homework.

Rewrite the sentence correctly: _____

_____

Apply the rule in a sentence of your own: _____

_____

WARM-UP 109   *Mark the errors:*

Of all the things my little sister does to bug me, breaking my toys hanging out in my room and tattling to Mom and Dad are the most annoying.

Rewrite the sentence correctly: _____

_____

Apply the rule in a sentence of your own: _____

_____

WARM-UP 110   *Mark the errors:*

I've lived in three countries: Mexico India and the United States.

Rewrite the sentence correctly: _____

_____

Apply the rule in a sentence of your own: _____

_____

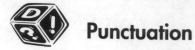

Punctuation

> **Use apostrophes to show possessives and contractions.**

See answers, page 195.

WARM-UP 111 *Mark the errors:*

The scorpions stinger is in its tail.

Rewrite the sentence correctly: _____

_____

Apply the rule in a sentence of your own: _____

_____

WARM-UP 112 *Mark the errors:*

Theyre nocturnal, so youre pretty safe from scorpions during the day.

Rewrite the sentence correctly: _____

_____

Apply the rule in a sentence of your own: _____

_____

WARM-UP 113   *Mark the errors:*

My schools Spider Club was formed last year by spider fans who wanted to learn all about scorpions unusual habits.

Rewrite the sentence correctly: _____

_____

Apply the rule in a sentence of your own: _____

_____

WARM-UP 114   *Mark the errors:*

Little has changed about the scorpions appearance in the last 300 million years.

Rewrite the sentence correctly: _____

_____

Apply the rule in a sentence of your own: _____

_____

WARM-UP 115   *Mark the errors:*

Its fascinating to learn that scorpions heads have four to twelve sets of eyes.

Rewrite the sentence correctly: _____

_____

Apply the rule in a sentence of your own: _____

_____

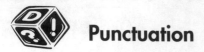

Punctuation

> **Use quotation marks to show dialogue and direct quotations.**

See answers, page 195.

WARM-UP 116   *Mark the errors:*

Brrrrr, Mary Sue shivered. It's the coldest day of the year.

Rewrite the sentence correctly: _____

_____

Apply the rule in a sentence of your own: _____

_____

WARM-UP 117   *Mark the errors:*

I'm turning up the heat this instant. It's freezing in here, she said.

Rewrite the sentence correctly: _____

_____

Apply the rule in a sentence of your own: _____

_____

WARM-UP 118   *Mark the errors:*

The newspaper's headline announced, Prepare for Below-Zero Temperatures!

Rewrite the sentence correctly: _____

_____

Apply the rule in a sentence of your own: _____

_____

WARM-UP 119   *Mark the errors:*

Mary Sue shook her head, muttering, I'm not stepping out of this house until spring.

Rewrite the sentence correctly: _____

_____

Apply the rule in a sentence of your own: _____

_____

WARM-UP 120   *Mark the errors:*

I can hardly wait for summer and warm weather, said Mary Sue to her friend Denise on the phone. We're going to have so much fun at the beach.

Rewrite the sentence correctly: _____

_____

Apply the rule in a sentence of your own: _____

Working With Individual

CONVENTIONS

Spelling

Punctuation

Capitalization

Grammar and Usage

CAPITALIZATION

- Did I always capitalize the pronoun *I* and the beginning of each sentence?

- Did I capitalize abbreviations and people's titles?

- Did I capitalize the important words in a title?

- Did I capitalize proper nouns for people, places, and things?

Photocopy for students to keep in their notebooks.

Rules to Remember FOR CAPITALIZATION

- Always capitalize the pronoun *I*.
  Example: *I wish I could go to Storyland every day.*

- Always put a capital at the beginning of each sentence, even in dialogue.
  Example: *The boy's father demanded, "Put that candy bar back in the dish!"*

- Capitalize abbreviations and people's titles.
  Example: *The current Miss America, who lives in Beaverton, OR, is a supporter of animal rights and member of the ASPCA.*

- Capitalize the first and last words and all other words of a title except articles (*a, an, the*), coordinating conjunctions (*and, but, or*), and prepositions with three letters or fewer (*at, to, for*).
  Example: *A Dachshund's Daring Day at the Dog Park*

- Capitalize proper nouns for people, places, organizations, and acronyms
  Example: *Mrs. Gadfly won a trip to Canada to attend the National Hockey League (NHL) playoffs.*

Add other important capitalization rules you want to remember here:

_____

_____

_____

_____

_____

_____

_____

Capitalization

> **Capitalize the pronoun *I* and the beginning of each sentence.**

See answers, page 196.

WARM-UP 121   *Mark the errors:*

in music class this week, i am going to learn how to play the guitar.

Rewrite the sentence correctly: _____

_____

Apply the rule in a sentence of your own: _____

_____

WARM-UP 122   *Mark the errors:*

how am i ever going to learn all of these chords for the guitar?

Rewrite the sentence correctly: _____

_____

Apply the rule in a sentence of your own: _____

_____

WARM-UP 123   *Mark the errors:*

i've been practicing a lot, so i'm really getting the hang of playing guitar.

Rewrite the sentence correctly: _____

_____

Apply the rule in a sentence of your own: _____

_____

WARM-UP 124   *Mark the errors:*

one day i hope to become a famous guitar player; i'll travel the world and entertain people everywhere.

Rewrite the sentence correctly: _____

_____

Apply the rule in a sentence of your own: _____

_____

WARM-UP 125   *Mark the errors:*

a famous guitarist whom i admire a lot is Stevie Ray Vaughan.

Rewrite the sentence correctly: _____

_____

Apply the rule in a sentence of your own: _____

_____

Capitalization

Capitalize abbreviations and people's titles.

See answers, page 196.

WARM-UP 126 *Mark the errors:*

mr. and mrs. Sanchez sent an rsvp to attend our wildlife fund raiser.

Rewrite the sentence correctly: _____

_____

Apply the rule in a sentence of your own: _____

_____

WARM-UP 127 *Mark the errors:*

I also heard from dr. Turner and governor Yee, who offered to help us.

Rewrite the sentence correctly: _____

_____

Apply the rule in a sentence of your own: _____

_____

WARM-UP 128 *Mark the errors:*

The manatee is on the endangered species list of the epa in Tallahassee, fl.

Rewrite the sentence correctly: _____

_____

Apply the rule in a sentence of your own: _____

_____

WARM-UP 129 *Mark the errors:*

I'll share research about the manatee habitat from professor Morrison of fsu.

Rewrite the sentence correctly: _____

_____

Apply the rule in a sentence of your own: _____

_____

WARM-UP 130 *Mark the errors:*

The Florida Fish and Wildlife Conservancy (fwc) has appointed ms. Lucas and Ed Thomas, jr., to be on the state fund-raising committee to save the manatee.

Rewrite the sentence correctly: _____

_____

Apply the rule in a sentence of your own: _____

_____

 **Capitalization**

> **Capitalize the important words in a title. (Remember to underline movie and book titles and put quotation marks around story titles.)**

See answers, page 197.

WARM-UP 131 *Mark the errors:*

My favorite book of all time is hatchet by Gary Paulsen.

Rewrite the sentence correctly: _____

_____

Apply the rule in a sentence of your own: _____

_____

WARM-UP 132 *Mark the errors:*

lord of the rings was a very popular book but an even more popular movie.

Rewrite the sentence correctly: _____

_____

Apply the rule in a sentence of your own: _____

_____

WARM-UP 133   *Mark the errors:*

When I was little, my favorite story was goldilocks and the three bears.

Rewrite the sentence correctly: _____

_____

Apply the rule in a sentence of your own: _____

_____

WARM-UP 134   *Mark the errors:*

On Saturdays, I can't wait to watch looney tunes cartoons.

Rewrite the sentence correctly: _____

_____

Apply the rule in a sentence of your own: _____

_____

WARM-UP 135   *Mark the errors:*

The best piece of writing that I worked on this year was a story called the amazing, marvelous, fantastic homework machine.

Rewrite the sentence correctly: _____

_____

Apply the rule in a sentence of your own: _____

_____

 **Capitalization**

> **Capitalize proper nouns for people, places, and things.**

See answers, page 197.

WARM-UP 136 *Mark the errors:*

This summer we're taking a road trip to visit aunt lanelle in california.

Rewrite the sentence correctly: _____

_____

Apply the rule in a sentence of your own: _____

_____

WARM-UP 137 *Mark the errors:*

We'll go through kansas, colorado, nevada, and new mexico and even stop in arizona to see the grand canyon.

Rewrite the sentence correctly: _____

_____

Apply the rule in a sentence of your own: _____

WARM-UP 138   *Mark the errors:*

uncle frank will be there, but my dad's sister vonda will be out of town.

Rewrite the sentence correctly: _____

_____

Apply the rule in a sentence of your own: _____

_____

WARM-UP 139   *Mark the errors:*

I hope we can go to disneyland and knott's berry farm while we're in southern california.

Rewrite the sentence correctly: _____

_____

Apply the rule in a sentence of your own: _____

_____

WARM-UP 140   *Mark the errors:*

Let's ask mom to stop at the nevada museum of gold mines in carson city.

Rewrite the sentence correctly: _____

_____

Apply the rule in a sentence of your own: _____

_____

Working With Individual

CONVENTIONS

Spelling

Punctuation

Capitalization

Grammar and Usage

GRAMMAR AND USAGE

- Did I use words correctly? (For example, homophones)

- Did I check verb tense and agreement?

- Have I used apostrophes to show possessives and contractions?

- Do my pronouns correctly name the person, place, or thing they stand for?

Photocopy for students to keep in their notebooks.

Rules to Remember FOR GRAMMAR AND USAGE

- Homophones, or words that sound alike but are spelled differently, are tricky. Check your work to make sure you have used common homophones correctly.
  Examples:
  People have a responsibility to put their dirty clothes in the right place.
  There is no way I would put my dirty socks on the table.
  They're right here, in my own dirty-clothes hamper.

- Verb tenses help show time in a piece of writing. For example, you would use verbs in the past tense to describe events that took place during the Civil War. The key to helping readers make sense of the time in your writing is using the tenses consistently.
  Examples:
  I walk to school in the morning and take the bus home. (present tense)
  I drove to the airport and flew to California. (past tense)

- Every subject and its verb must also be in agreement, so that singular and plural nouns are matched to verbs with correct endings.
  Example:
  Dogs love chocolate but it makes them sick. (*dogs love* = plural; *it makes* = singular)

- Apostrophes can be used to show possesives and contractions.
  Examples:
  Bailey's favorite pastime is sleeping on my bed, curled up with my other cat.
  It's a nice life if you're a cat.

- Pronouns and their antecedents (the word they stand for) should always agree. The pronouns *who, what,* and *that* can show relationships in a sentence when they're used correctly. Make sure that you
  (a) match the pronoun with its antecedent;
  (b) use *who* to refer to specific people and animals with names;
  (c) use *what* to refer to inanimate objects;
  (d) use *that* to refer to generic animals, things, and people, too.
  Examples:
  The man was snoring so loudly, he woke up the entire bus depot.
  Mr. Rimbaldi, who was snoring, made everyone laugh out loud.
  What is that funny sound Mr. Rimbaldi is making?
  I've heard a lot of snores in my life, but that really takes the cake.

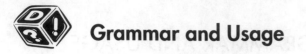

Grammar and Usage

> **Use words correctly (For example, homophones).**

See answers, page 198.

WARM-UP 141   *Mark the errors:*

When you go to Washington, D.C., their are many things to
see they're.

Rewrite the sentences correctly: _____

_____

Apply the rule in a sentence of your own: _____

_____

WARM-UP 142   *Mark the errors:*

Visiting a monument? I advice you to stand stationery and take in
the cite.

Rewrite the sentence correctly: _____

_____

Apply the rule in a sentence of your own: _____

_____

WARM-UP 143   *Mark the errors:*

Whose to know how many tourists visit? No one, accept the
park service.

Rewrite the sentences correctly: _____

_____

Apply the rule in a sentence of your own: _____

_____

WARM-UP 144   *Mark the errors:*

I was to overcome with awe to notice too of the smaller side exhibits.

Rewrite the sentence correctly: _____

_____

Apply the rule in a sentence of your own: _____

_____

WARM-UP 145   *Mark the errors:*

You're favorite monument might be different than mine, but your entitled to
you're own choice.

Rewrite the sentence correctly: _____

_____

Apply the rule in a sentence of your own: _____

_____

Grammar and Usage

> **Check verb tense and agreement.**

See answers, page 198.

WARM-UP 146 *Mark the errors:*

Last summer I have a part-time job, but it is hard work and takes a lot of time.

Rewrite the sentence correctly: _____

_____

Apply the rule in a sentence of your own: _____

_____

WARM-UP 147 *Mark the errors:*

Jobs like baby-sitting builded self-confidence and develops self-esteem.

Rewrite the sentence correctly: _____

_____

Apply the rule in a sentence of your own: _____

_____

WARM-UP 148   *Mark the errors:*

When you wanted to buy CDs, clothes, or other items, you are needing your own spending money.

Rewrite the sentence correctly: _____

_____

Apply the rule in a sentence of your own: _____

_____

WARM-UP 149   *Mark the errors:*

To getting a good job, you need to has a good personality and been a good worker.

Rewrite the sentence correctly: _____

_____

Apply the rule in a sentence of your own: _____

_____

WARM-UP 150   *Mark the errors:*

Everything you did in life can leads to success if you tries 100 percent.

Rewrite the sentence correctly: _____

_____

Apply the rule in a sentence of your own: _____

_____

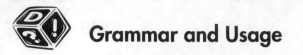

Grammar and Usage

> **Use apostrophes to show possessives and contractions.**

See answers, page 199.

WARM-UP 151   *Mark the errors:*

Stars are billion's and billion's of mile's away.

Rewrite the sentence correctly: _____

_____

Apply the rule in a sentence of your own: _____

_____

WARM-UP 152   *Mark the errors:*

I found a Web site where you can name a star after yourself: Josephs star. Who wouldnt want to do that?

*Rewrite the sentences correctly:*_____

_____

Apply the rule in a sentence of your own: _____

_____

WARM-UP 153   *Mark the errors:*

Its hard to imagine how we could travel fast enough to reach the stars'.

Rewrite the sentence correctly: _____

_____

Apply the rule in a sentence of your own: _____

_____

WARM-UP 154   *Mark the errors:*

At night, I watch for moving star's; those are actually satellites'.

Rewrite the sentence correctly: _____

_____

Apply the rule in a sentence of your own: _____

_____

WARM-UP 155   *Mark the errors:*

Of all the star's, I like the sun the most because its the brightest.

Rewrite the sentence correctly: _____

_____

Apply the rule in a sentence of your own: _____

_____

 **Grammar and Usage**

> Make sure pronouns correctly name the person, place, or thing they stand for.

See answers, page 199.

WARM-UP 156 *Mark the errors:*

My female cat Bailey, what is orange with white stripes, enjoys lying in the sun on his back.

Rewrite the sentence correctly: _____

_____

Apply the rule in a sentence of your own: _____

_____

WARM-UP 157 *Mark the errors:*

Laura, the girl what is going to feed my cat while I am gone, is going to come over on its way to school each day.

Rewrite the sentence correctly: _____

_____

Apply the rule in a sentence of your own: _____

_____

WARM-UP 158   *Mark the errors:*

Bailey steals my brother's toys and hides it where he can't be found.

Rewrite the sentence correctly: _____

_____

Apply the rule in a sentence of your own: _____

_____

WARM-UP 159   *Mark the errors:*

If you pet it, Bailey rolls over like a dog what likes their belly scratched.

Rewrite the sentence correctly: _____

_____

Apply the rule in a sentence of your own: _____

_____

WARM-UP 160   *Mark the errors:*

How that cat makes me laugh! I'm glad I have them to keep my family and I company.

Rewrite the sentence correctly: _____

_____

Apply the rule in a sentence of your own: _____

_____

Working With Multiple Conventions

Use the editor's marks to correct the sentences below. The number of errors you should try to find is indicated after each sentence. Then use your corrected sentences to create a well-edited, indented paragraph on a separate sheet of paper.

The fall tv shows this year sounds terific. (3)

There are so many different kinds that Im sure Ill find a new show who I really like. (3)

Maybe their will be a new Sportscaster who enjoys College football as much as me. (4)

One thing Im not looking forward to about the fall seeson are all the knew comercials. (5)

it seems as if they're more and more every year (3)

(Continues with Warm-Up 162.)

Check It!

- Is my spelling correct?
- Does punctuation guide the reader through the text?
- Have I capitalized correctly?
- Have I checked my grammar and usage?

See answers, page 200, and editor's marks, page 119.

Working With Multiple Conventions

Use the editor's marks to correct the sentences below. The number of errors you should try to find is indicated after each sentence. Then use your corrected sentences to create a well-edited, indented paragraph on a separate sheet of paper.

1 day i timed a half-hour tv show and it were only 19 minuts long after subtracting all the comercials. (6)

Its terible how much time is wastd on comercials. (4)

Most of the time I went to the kitchin to get some thing to eat rather than watch more comerceals. (4)

Their are a few good wons that make you laff (4)

tv should have more comercials that is entertaining, like those played during the super bowl. (6)

Check It!

- Is my spelling correct?

- Does punctuation guide the reader through the text?

- Have I capitalized correctly?

- Have I checked my grammar and usage?

See answers, page 200, and editor's marks, page 119.

Working With Multiple Conventions

Use the editor's marks to correct the sentences below. The number of errors you should try to find is indicated after each sentence. Then use your corrected sentences to create a well-edited, indented paragraph on a separate sheet of paper.

when you travel its hard to find a decent restarant. (3)

There is many places to choose from, but most of it serve fast food, and Id realy rather have a good hot meel (6)

Its important to have a helthy meel at the end of a longday in the car with my family. (4)

beleive me, it can be exhausting driveing with them. (3)

One thing Ive noticd is that there arent as many family-stile restarants as fast-food places along the hiway. (6)

(Continues with Warm-Up 164.)

Check It!

- Is my spelling correct?
- Does punctuation guide the reader through the text?
- Have I capitalized correctly?
- Have I checked my grammar and usage?

See answers, pages 200–201, and editor's marks, page 119.

Working With Multiple Conventions

Use the editor's marks to correct the sentences below. The number of errors you should try to find is indicated after each sentence. Then use your corrected sentences to create a well-edited, indented paragraph on a separate sheet of paper.

It culd be that runing and maintaning them is more expensive. (4)

or it could be that there not as poppular with toursts. (4)

Perhaps their hard to find 'cuz you cant get to them easyly from the hi way. (5)

Regardless of the reseon, i still look carfully for a good 1 to eat in with my family (5)

The rite restarant will hav things we like, and their will be healthy menu choiyces (6)

Check It!

- Is my spelling correct?
- Does punctuation guide the reader through the text?
- Have I capitalized correctly?
- Have I checked my grammar and usage?

See answers, page 201, and editor's marks, page 119.

Working With Multiple Conventions

Use the editor's marks to correct the sentences below. The number of errors you should try to find is indicated after each sentence. Then use your corrected sentences to create a well-edited, indented paragraph on a separate sheet of paper.

one of the hardst things about being the youngist in the family is that no 1 thinks me can do anything by myself. (5)

No won beleives that Im old enough to make her own decisions or do anything on her own (6)

when my older brother want to do things with friends, my Mom and dad say, sure. (6)

But when I ask to do the same things they say, no, your to young. (5)

Sometimes I think they were afraid that if they let me make decisions or go out by yourself, they are admiting that their youngest child is growwing up. (4)

(Continues with Warm-Up 166.)

Check It!

- Is my spelling correct?
- Does punctuation guide the reader through the text?
- Have I checked my grammar and usage?
- Have I capitalized correctly?

See answers, page 201, and editor's marks, page 119.

Working With Multiple Conventions

Use the editor's marks to correct the sentences below. The number of errors you should try to find is indicated after each sentence. Then use your corrected sentences to create a well-edited, indented paragraph on a separate sheet of paper.

My parents' definitly do'nt want to admit that I was growing up. (4)

but its not fare to me (4)

I want to have sum fredome, to. (3)

Id be responsible and show they that Im worthy, if theyd only give me a chance (5)

younger kids deserve a chance to does things on his own, two. (4)

Check It!

- Is my spelling correct?
- Does punctuation guide the reader through the text?
- Have I capitalized correctly?
- Have I checked my grammar and usage?

See answers, page 202, and editor's marks, page 119.

Working With Multiple Conventions

Use the editor's marks to correct the sentences below. The number of errors you should try to find is indicated after each sentence. Then use your corrected sentences to create a well-edited, indented paragraph on a separate sheet of paper.

A individual from History I realy admire is abraham lincoln (6)

he is an intresting person and a Great president, to. (5)

It musta been very hard back in the 1860S to fight aganst all the peopl which wanted to kepe slavery. (6)

But if lincoln hadnt be strong and stood up for his beleifs, we wood not have abolished slavery. (5)

he was the rite man to be President of the united states' at the time. (6)

(Continues with Warm-Up 168.)

Check It!

- Is my spelling correct?

- Does punctuation guide the reader through the text?

- Have I capitalized correctly?

- Have I checked my grammar and usage?

See answers, page 202, and editor's marks, page 119.

Working With Multiple Conventions

Use the editor's marks to correct the sentences below. The number of errors you should try to find is indicated after each sentence. Then use your corrected sentences to create a well-edited, indented paragraph on a separate sheet of paper.

As a person in todays world, I really admire abraham lincoln becaus he had a hard life. (4)

But he didnt let its problums hold he back. (4)

Comeing from a small town and being very poor when He was young did not stop him from becomeing one of the most important people in american History. (5)

he had a strong caracter and respected peopl as individual's. (4)

his life storey is interesting and enspiring to youngpeople like I. (5)

Check It!

- Is my spelling correct?
- Does punctuation guide the reader through the text?
- Have I capitalized correctly?
- Have I checked my grammar and usage?

See answers, page 202, and editor's marks, page 119.

Working With Multiple Conventions

Use the editor's marks to correct the sentences below. The number of errors you should try to find is indicated after each sentence. Then use your corrected sentences to create a well-edited, indented paragraph on a separate sheet of paper.

my parents think I should keeps mine room spotlessly cleen (5)

I disagrae. i sae it's my room and it should bee how I like it. (4)

However, thay make me cleen it ever weak end, whether I like it or not (6)

Its not fun atAll, let me tell u. (4)

I had to pick up all my clothes, put away my games and toyz restack my books on the shelfs and dust and vacume (7)

(Continues with Warm-Up 170.)

Check It!

- Is my spelling correct?

- Does punctuation guide the reader through the text?

- Have I capitalized correctly?

- Have I checked my grammar and usage?

See answers, page 203, and editor's marks, page 119.

Working With Multiple Conventions

Use the editor's marks to correct the sentences below. The number of errors you should try to find is indicated after each sentence. Then use your corrected sentences to create a well-edited, indented paragraph on a separate sheet of paper.

then I hav ta wash my sheats and re make my bed (6)

Their is a lot to do every weak end 'cuz I dont do much during the weak. (6)

What really bugs' me is that cents im the oldest, i hav to do the work all by myselves. (7)

My Mom and Dad help my litle brothers and sisters—that's' not fare. (5)

Dont tell them I told you this, But when my room is finaly cleen i realy like it. (6)

Check It!

- Is my spelling correct?

- Does punctuation guide the reader through the text?

- Have I capitalized correctly?

- Have I checked my grammar and usage?

See answers, page 203, and editor's marks, page 119.

Working With Multiple Conventions

Use the editor's marks to correct the sentences below. The number of errors you should try to find is indicated after each sentence. Then use your corrected sentences to create a well-edited, indented paragraph on a separate sheet of paper.

Skatebording can be an Art a Hobby a Sport, or just a way to get around conveniently. (6)

some peopl call it a extreem sport because it is so creativ. (5)

In 2002, a report from the marketing research firm american sports' data revealed that their were 12.5 million skateboarders in the world. (5)

Eigty percent of those Skateboarder's were under the age of 18, & 74 percent is mail. (6)

Skate Boarding are a sport that has really taken of in the last 20 yeers. (5)

(Continues with Warm-Up 172.)

Check It!

- Is my spelling correct?
- Does punctuation guide the reader through the text?
- Have I capitalized correctly?
- Have I checked my grammar and usage?

See answers, page 203, and editor's marks, page 119.

Working With Multiple Conventions

Use the editor's marks to correct the sentences below. The number of errors you should try to find is indicated after each sentence. Then use your corrected sentences to create a well-edited, indented paragraph on a separate sheet of paper.

The strete is the place of choyce for todays Skate boarders'. (6)

the boords and wheel's are very lite comparet to the early verzions. (6)

since the 1990s, tho, skatboards isn't changed that much (4)

Their are many skate board parks in city's across the countrie where skate boarders can freestyle skate and try out exciting new moves on Ramps and vertical drops. (6)

the Ollie is the basis for many triks, but the Flip was todays most popular move. (5)

Check It!

- Is my spelling correct?

- Does punctuation guide the reader through the text?

- Have I capitalized correctly?

- Have I checked my grammar and usage?

See answers, page 204, and editor's marks, page 119.

Working With Multiple Conventions

Use the editor's marks to correct the sentences below. The number of errors you should try to find is indicated after each sentence. Then use your corrected sentences to create a well-edited, indented paragraph on a separate sheet of paper.

1 of the things Id change at my school is the rule about Not Eating in clas (6)

i think it is realy hard to sit still all day and not had any thing to eat. (4)

Kids nede snaks to give them—Energy 4 Learning. (6)

If they're was a time in the morning for snack, for instence, than everyone could have a quik byte, feel better, and be Ready to Learn more right away. (7)

their would have to be rule's abowt witch snaks would work, though. (6)

(Continues with Warm-Up 174.)

Check It!

- Is my spelling correct?

- Does punctuation guide the reader through the text?

- Have I capitalized correctly?

- Have I checked my grammar and usage?

See answers, page 204, and editor's marks, page 119.

Working With Multiple Conventions

Use the editor's marks to correct the sentences below. The number of errors you should try to find is indicated after each sentence. Then use your corrected sentences to create a well-edited, indented paragraph on a separate sheet of paper.

For egsample, you could'nt have a Snack that needed refrigeration or heeting. (4)

But you could has a snack like a piece of fruit some cheese and crackers or a Granola Bar. (5)

these kinds' of snacks wood be easy to prepare and simple to dispose of when your finished. (4)

Kid's would haf to clean up after Snack Time and not leaves extra food lying around (6)

It could be fun healthy and an good way to break up the day if we were allowwed to have snack's at school. (5)

Check It!

- Is my spelling correct?
- Does punctuation guide the reader through the text?
- Have I capitalized correctly?
- Have I checked my grammar and usage?

See answers, pages 204–205, and editor's marks, page 119.

Working With Multiple Conventions

Use the editor's marks to correct the sentences below. The number of errors you should try to find is indicated after each sentence. Then use your corrected sentences to create a well-edited, indented paragraph on a separate sheet of paper.

Becomeing a Teacher is alot of hard work and takes meny year's of Study. (6)

They are a wonder ful job, however, 'cuz you get to help kids' lern. (6)

what culd possibly be moore rewarding then that (5)

Although their are many difficult things to learn to be a good Teacher, its a very worthwhile Profesion. (5)

helping a New Generation learn how to read & rite is an awesome responsibility and alot of fun, to. (7)

(Continues with Warm-Up 176.)

Check It!

- Is my spelling correct?
- Does punctuation guide the reader through the text?
- Have I capitalized correctly?
- Have I checked my grammar and usage?

See answers, page 205, and editor's marks, page 119.

Working With Multiple Conventions

Use the editor's marks to correct the sentences below. The number of errors you should try to find is indicated after each sentence. Then use your corrected sentences to create a well-edited, indented paragraph on a separate sheet of paper.

What would you wants to do if you where a teacher. (3)

Id want to teach art, and paint from september to joon. (4)

My students will probably like to work with clay collage and printmaking, too (4)

Sculptur in 3 dimensions would be one of many exsiting activitys. (4)

I bet he culd build the Brooklyn bridge from woodin sticks and gloo. (5)

Check It!

- Is my spelling correct?
- Does punctuation guide the reader through the text?
- Have I capitalized correctly?
- Have I checked my grammar and usage?

See answers, page 205, and editor's marks, page 119.

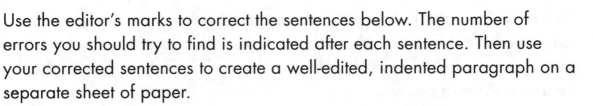

Working With Multiple Conventions

Use the editor's marks to correct the sentences below. The number of errors you should try to find is indicated after each sentence. Then use your corrected sentences to create a well-edited, indented paragraph on a separate sheet of paper.

last year there was two earthquakes you could really feel in san Francisco. (3)

I know because my friends cusin lives their. (3)

She calls california the shaek-n-bake state because they are so many earthquakes and it was so hot. (4)

buildings has to be bilt to a special code to make sure their stable. (4)

Otherwise, theyl just crumbled into dust (3)

(Continues with Warm-Up 178.)

Check It!

- Is my spelling correct?
- Does punctuation guide the reader through the text?
- Have I capitalized correctly?
- Have I checked my grammar and usage?

See answers, page 206, and editor's marks, page 119.

Working With Multiple Conventions

Use the editor's marks to correct the sentences below. The number of errors you should try to find is indicated after each sentence. Then use your corrected sentences to create a well-edited, indented paragraph on a separate sheet of paper.

I am greatful that I live far away from they're, but were still in a quake zone. (3)

Me and my dad have practised earthquake drills by hideing in the bathtub or standing in a sturdie dorrway. (6)

Its not save to go outside during an Earthquake even if you wants to get away from the bilding (6)

if you are at schol durring an earthquake, you should take cover under you're desk (5)

You should always have lots of fresh watter a radeo and caned food ready incase of an emergency. (6)

Check It!

- Is my spelling correct?
- Does punctuation guide the reader through the text?
- Have I capitalized correctly?
- Have I checked my grammar and usage?

See answers, page 206, and editor's marks, page 119.

Working With Multiple Conventions

Use the editor's marks to correct the sentences below. The number of errors you should try to find is indicated after each sentence. Then use your corrected sentences to create a well-edited, indented paragraph on a separate sheet of paper.

Its so hard togo to bed wen my parents tell me too (5)

i try hard to fall asleep, but its not easy when its still light out or when im not tyred. (6)

Sometimes I hid a book under the covers and read latee in to the nyght (5)

I turns the light out really fast if I here my Mom or dad comming to chek on me (6)

with the covers puled up, I try to breathe normaly until them have left the room, and than I go back to reading untill I fall asleep. (6)

(Continues with Warm-Up 180.)

Check It!

- Is my spelling correct?
- Does punctuation guide the reader through the text?
- Have I capitalized correctly?
- Have I checked my grammar and usage?

See answers, page 206–207, and editor's marks, page 119.

Working With Multiple Conventions

Use the editor's marks to correct the sentences below. The number of errors you should try to find is indicated after each sentence. Then use your corrected sentences to create a well-edited, indented paragraph on a separate sheet of paper.

in addition to new bedtime rules, their should be a rulle againgst home work. (5)

if you work realy hard at school all day, you shouldnt have to do moore work at home. (4)

Two much homework could makke you're brane so tired they mite wear out. (6)

if all you do are homework everie night, you don't had enuf time to play outside with you're friends (7)

Kids shouldnt have to much work to do at home because then they wont get to due all the fun things that are good for them todo. (5)

Check It!

- Is my spelling correct?
- Does punctuation guide the reader through the text?
- Have I checked my grammar and usage?
- Have I capitalized correctly?

See answers, page 207, and editor's marks, page 119.

Conventions

The Mechanical Correctness
of the Piece

Punctuation smoothly guides the reader.
The grammar contributes to clarity and style.

Capitals are handled well. "Clean copy."
Paragraphing complements the organization.

Spelling is mostly correct—even on harder words.
Only light editing is needed—at the most.

Ready to share!

5

My spelling is correct on common words.

Simple things are done well.

Paragraphing was attempted.

My errors are consistent.

4

Halfway home!

There are minor problems in
grammar/usage. I hastily edited.

3

Punctuation is basically correct.

Capitals are correct at the beginning of sentences
and names, but not in trickier places.

2

Just beginning

There are numerous errors. I couldn't publish this yet.

Paragraphing is random or not present.

1

Errors are extremely distracting. This piece is not edited.

Struggling. The reader has to translate to get meaning.

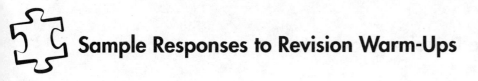

Sample Responses to Revision Warm-Ups

The following answers are *suggested* responses. Accept all responses that aim to revise the examples according to the specific trait focus stated in the directions.

Finding a Topic

1. Little brothers can be so irritating sometimes. Just yesterday, Jerome, my three-year-old brother, got into my closet and used colored markers on my best white athletic shoes to give them "style." He's a pest and my parents should do something about him.

2. When my mom and dad said we were going to see Mount Rushmore, I thought, "Oh no! That sounds terribly boring." Who would have dreamed that four 60-foot-tall heads of presidents, carved out of granite, could be so awesome that when it was time to leave, we couldn't be pried away?

3. I was confident I could cook the best cake ever for my brother's birthday. I combined the chocolate cake mix with the milk and egg and then poured the mix into the cake pan and let it cook for the recommended time and temperature. But after it cooled, when I tried to take it out of the pan, I realized I forgot to grease the pan first, so the cake came out in chunks. I used chocolate frosting to glue it all together. It may not have been pretty, but it sure did taste good.

4. Sometimes something happens in science that gets the world's attention. The demotion of Pluto from a planet to a "dwarf planet" was such an event. As scientists from around the country met to decide the fate of Pluto, many people, including publishers, stood by anxiously waiting. This decision would mean changing a lot of books and exhibits in science museums everywhere. A single decision like demoting Pluto's status as a planet has had a ripple effect around the world.

Focusing the Topic

5. I huddle under a blanket in front of the fireplace, listening to the trees outside make scraping noises against the side of the house, afraid someone is breaking in. I stare at the doorknob, willing it not to move.

6. Vincent van Gogh created more than 900 paintings from 1881 to 1890. One of his best known, *Irises*, sold for $49 million in 1987. Just imagine: van Gogh painted more than 90 pictures in the last two months of his life, many of which turned out to be his most famous.

7. Rain forests, such as those in Brazil's dense, warm wetlands, are home for millions of plants and animals and vital to the ecology of the planet Earth. The plants in rain forests generate much of the Earth's oxygen, and they are also useful in developing new drugs to fight illness and disease. There's no end to the benefit of the rain forests. Tragically, we might be seeing an end to rain forests on the planet.

8. Poor Pluto. Once considered the smallest planet in the solar system, it is now scratched from the list. In August 2006, a group of astronomers decided that since Pluto is so small, and since it doesn't clear its own orbit, it should be called a "dwarf planet." Not everyone agrees, but for now, this is how it's going to be for Pluto, a frozen "dwarf planet" of whirling ice and rocks.

Developing the Topic

9. The first day of summer vacation is the best. When you wake up, you get dressed really quickly, before your mom knows you are up, so you can sneak outside to find your friends. You don't want her to catch you and make you do chores. Boring! So, you quietly unlatch the kitchen door and dart outside to spend the day building a fort, playing catch, and spinning on the old tire swing in the backyard.

10. It's almost impossible to tip a cow without her knowing what's up. Cows have excellent hearing and are easily awakened, so it's hard to sneak up on them. Actually, cows don't sleep standing up. Most take naps lying down, so it is hard to even catch a cow unaware if you wanted to try to tip one over.

11. When you wake up and hear the rain coming down outside, you might think it's going to be a wet, cold, and boring day. But there are lots of fun things you can do on a rainy day. You can build a fort out of blankets and chairs. You can grab a new magazine or book and curl up by the fireplace and read. You can bake cookies and fill the air with their yummy, delicious smell. Try doing something new on a rainy day; you might surprise yourself with how much fun you can have!

12. Until it was recently demoted to "dwarf planet" status, Pluto was the smallest planet in our solar system, taking 248.5 Earth years to orbit the sun. Discovered in 1930 by Clyde W. Tombaugh at Lowell Observatory in Arizona, it was named after the Greek lord of the underworld. The first spacecraft to try to reach Pluto, New Horizons, was launched in January 2006. If all goes well, it should reach Pluto in 2015. If and when it reaches the brown dwarf planet, the spaceship will find that it's cold there, very cold at -390 degrees Fahrenheit.

Using Details

13. Worn smooth by the rough tumbling of the ocean waves against the grainy sand, this little seashell fit perfectly into the palm of my hand. It was a soft pink, and it had a shiny, iridescent core where its original owner, a little sea creature, once lived.

14. During the final six brutal hours of Hurricane Carlene last August, buildings collapsed, roads washed out, and power lines snapped like twigs in the 100-mile-an-hour winds. The scene had a surreal quality, like something from a science fiction movie. But it wasn't a movie; it was what was left of my hometown.

15. What a scare I got while walking home from my friend's house last Saturday evening. I heard something following me, which sent a chill up my spine. What if a bad person was trying to catch me? I sped up, but so did the sounds behind me. Now I was really nervous. I started to sprint toward my house, hoping I'd make it before whoever it was caught me. Right when I got to the front door, I reached for the handle and turned around, expecting to see someone very close by, about to grab me. He jumped up on me all right, but then he licked my face. It was my neighbor's dog!

16. Once thought to be the smallest planet in our solar system, this tiny body made of ice and rocks and that orbits around the sun is the center of a new controversy. Is it a planet, or isn't it? That's up for debate. Its tiny size, compared with that of its larger neighbors, Neptune and Jupiter, and the fact that it hasn't cleared its own orbit have made its classification the subject of debate and study since its discovery in 1930.

Creating the Lead

17. It felt like I'd snagged a whale—the fishing pole was nearly bent in half, and I had to holler for help to keep from losing my grip on this enormous prize catch.

18. Eating slimy foods that make you gag. Finding secret treasure clues. Trying to get from Bangkok to New York City with no money. You never know what to expect next from my favorite reality show.

19. Yawn, stretch, yawn. It's really hard to get going today. I stayed up until after midnight and didn't get my full eight hours. Now I'm paying for that decision!

20. Just like Judith Viorst's character Alexander, I had a horrible, terrible, awful, very bad day last Monday. Everything I touched went sour. First, my alarm clock didn't go off, so I missed my early morning wrestling practice. The coach is making me come in over the weekend to make it up—ugh. Then, the bus got a flat tire, and we were stuck on the side of the road for an hour until another bus driver came to help. And finally, as if that weren't enough, I left all my homework, which I had finished the night before, at home, on the kitchen table. Argh. And all that happened before noon.

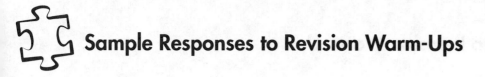

Sample Responses to Revision Warm-Ups

Using Sequence Words

21. Once it started to rain, we got soaked to the skin. So we ran into the building for shelter and had to stay there for hours while the thunder and lightning storm raged on.

22. First I opened the package and poured the cake mix into the bowl. Next, I cracked open the egg, added water, and then mixed all the ingredients together. Then, I baked the cake and finally, I got to eat it—yummy!

23. After I wrote the first draft of my story I reread it to myself to find any mistakes or places where it didn't make sense. Sure enough, I found some places to revise and made the story a lot stronger. Then, I read my revised version out loud to a friend and found one more place to revise. Finally, I edited my story for conventions so I could publish it and share it with the whole class.

24. Do you ever have days when you wish you hadn't gotten out of bed? That's how my day was last Monday. At first I thought I was just in a lousy mood and that's why bad things kept happening. But then my bad mood spilled over to my mom when I didn't like the breakfast she made me and it hurt her feelings. Another thing that was upsetting was when my dog ran after the neighbor's cat and Mrs. Kuvluc yelled at poor Marco. Finally, the day was over. I was happy to have another chance to have a better day on Tuesday.

Developing the Body

25. The day my mom told me we were going to move was really sad. I knew it would be hard saying good-bye to my friends. But soon, boxes were everywhere, and I was packing up all my stuff. I wrapped my trophies carefully so they wouldn't break. Then, we watched as all our boxes were loaded onto the truck, and they were off, off to our new place, new life, and maybe some new trophies.

26. To begin the metamorphosis, the adult female butterfly lays eggs on plants. Out of these eggs hatch larvae, or caterpillars, that eat and eat and eat. Once they are full grown, they attach to a place on a leaf or twig, or are buried underground and go into hibernation as a chrysalis. Finally, the butterfly hatches, and it can fly away into its adult life.

27. Recycling may take a little extra time, but it helps the environment. It cuts down on waste because recycled items are reused to make new products. Two of the easiest items to recycle are glass and cans. At our school you put the glass in blue bins and cans in red bins, and they are taken by staff to the recycle center once a week. This way, we're doing our small part to maintain the Earth's resources but we could do more. I think we should recycle paper next!

28. I was having the worst day ever. The bus to school arrived late and was completely full. When I got on, there was hardly any room for me to sit, and I had to put my backpack on my lap and squeeze into a seat that already had two people sitting on it. And it was Jess and David, of all people, two guys I'm not crazy about. They shot me dirty looks the whole way to school and threatened to take my backpack and empty it out into the aisle of the bus so all my stuff would get scattered about. I was so happy to finally get to school safely, in one piece, with my backpack. "What else is going to happen today to make it terrible?" I thought to myself as I ran inside, away from Jess and David, to the safety of the school. "Oh, no! I've already missed my favorite class."

Ending With a Sense of Resolution

29. b) And from that day on we never forgot about the little dancing figurine that mysteriously disappeared from the living room that fateful winter day. Were we just imagining it, or did the statue do a little pirouette and wink at us just before it vanished from right under our noses? It was always in the back of our minds, even when we grew up and moved away.

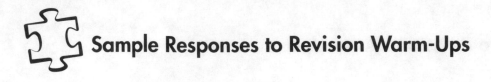

30. The next time you are in the voting booth, look around. Are you so sure that the person standing next to you shouldn't be a kid my age? After all, the people you are electing and the laws you are voting on affect me as much as you.

31. As it turns out, tarantulas are not nearly as scary as they appear. They rarely bite humans, and when they do, it's not poisonous, just mildly irritating. Still, soft and furry though they may be, I'd still rather curl up with my dog than a tarantula. My dog doesn't paralyze and consume its prey with fangs that secrete digestive juices. Slurp.

32. b) Can someone wave a magic wand and let me do last Monday over? I never want to repeat that awful day again!
c) Even my dog, Marco, seemed happy that the day was over. His tail was wagging as we snuggled in for the night, ready for better dreams of Tuesday.

Establishing a Tone

33. (*nervous, anxious, worried, edgy*) The night before I went bungee jumping for the first time, I couldn't sleep a bit. Why had I promised my friends I'd go with them? Was I out of my mind? My hands were so clammy, and the sheets felt soggy where I gripped them—as if hanging on to them would save me tomorrow. Tomorrow. My heart was racing, my legs were jumping, and I knew, I just knew I was going to throw up before this was all over.

34. (*authoritative, informed, confident, knowledgeable*) Imagine how different our country would be today if Abraham Lincoln had not been president. His steadfast belief in the strength of this nation to unite during the most difficult of times can be summed up in his second inaugural address: "With malice toward none; with charity for all; with firmness in the right, as God gives us to see the right, let us strive on to finish the work we are in; to bind up the nation's wounds."

35. (*confident, firm, patriotic, certain*) In just a few short years, I'm going to be standing in the voting booth casting my ballot for a man or a woman who will have the power to make things better or worse for our country. Voting is an awesome right and responsibility that Americans should not take for granted. Think of it: We get to choose who leads. In our country it is up to the people—you and me—to make these important decisions. Free elections are part of what makes this country great. So although many young people don't exercise their voting rights, I won't be in that group. I'll be first in line when I'm eligible to vote. Count on it.

36. Oh, my aching back. I wish I'd listened to my dad when he warned me that my new backpack was too large. Now, with it full of books and assignments, I can barely carry it. I'm hunched and scrunched, and I have to stagger from one class to the next. I guess I better fess up to my dad and ask if he'd mind getting me a new, smaller one, so I can survive this year. One good thing though if a strong wind comes up, I won't blow away as long as I have this huge weight holding me down!

Conveying the Purpose

37. (narrative) I'll never forget the day I got my first bike. It was Christmas, and snowing, and I wanted to ride it so badly. I ached to ride that shiny new two-wheeler, with its banana seat, woven flowered basket, and the bell that I couldn't keep my hands off. It was hot pink. My mom told me I'd have to wait until the pavement was bare and dry. At the rate the snow was falling, it felt like it would be July before I'd get to ride the bike of my dreams.

38. (expository) Did you know certain frogs can jump 20 feet in a single leap? Did you know frogs absorb water through their skin so they don't need to drink? Did you know the smallest frogs in the world are less than half an inch long? Frogs are fascinating amphibians!

39. (persuasive) The grumbling started the first day Mr. Boudreau gave us homework. It continued every day after, as we were assigned to read long books, do complex math problems, and learn how to apply scientific principles. And I'll admit, I wasn't really happy about working that hard, either. That is, until a few months went by and I realized how much we were learning and how fast. Mr. Boudreau, though tough and challenging, made learning hard material fun and found time to help everyone "work smart," as he liked to say. I only wish all kids had a chance to be in his class. He's the kind of teacher you never forget.

40. Backpacks help kids keep their books and materials close by and handy at school. However, because some of the books students are carrying are so heavy, backpacks are getting unwieldy for kids and causing back injuries. When children carry more than 30 percent of their body weight on their backs, the strain may cause long-term problems. If kids are going to use backpacks, the loaded packs should never weigh more than ten pounds, and they should have well-designed shoulder straps so they are as comfortable as possible. After all, kids don't need more than ten pounds of homework at any given time anyway, right?

Creating a Connection to the Audience

41. We had a golden retriever when I was little, and I have such fond memories of Miska. I remember rolling around on the floor with her every evening—fur flying in every direction—until inevitably, we'd break something, and my parents would yell at us both to "knock it off!" We'd slink out of the room together, out the back door, and run and chase outside until it was finally time to go to bed.

42. c) To a police office: "I was skating on the ramp and sidewalk. I hope that's okay. I've got pads just in case I fall, so I don't hurt myself."

43. Dear Principal:

I am writing about a concern I have regarding the school rule which forbids students to wear hats. I'm not sure when this rule started or why, but in today's world, it isn't considered rude or offensive to wear a hat. Actually, it's quite the opposite: it's a statement of style. Also there's another advantage for students coming from gym class or who just didn't get around to taking a shower. In the words of Julia Roberts, Academy Award-winning actress: "I enjoy hats. And when one has filthy hair, that is a good accessory." Please consider lifting this ban on hats at our school and make it possible for students to assert their individuality.

Sincerely, A Hat-Loving Student

44. I bet you were buying school supplies yesterday, just like I was. Do you like to find exactly the right thing? I sure do. I was looking all over Shop-a-Lot to find the perfect cobalt blue backpack that I'd seen earlier this week. I had my heart set on buying it on my back-to-school shopping trip. The backpack had soft, squishy shoulder pads and the most awesome secret-zipper places to store all my stuff. But as I looked all over, I couldn't believe it wasn't there. Was every one of them sold already? Then I looked down one more aisle, and I saw it. There was just one left. I started running, my hands outstretched, and I grabbed it before anyone else could. It was mine. The perfect backpack was all mine!

Taking Risks to Create Voice

45. It was a rip-snortin' firecrackin' holiday this year for the Fourth of July. After shooting off all our fireworks and listening to my mom say, "Be careful. You'll put your eyes out!" about a bazillion times, we cleaned up and went into the house for some tasty homemade ice cream. It was my favorite: chocolate-huckleberry with a little lemon zest. Yummm!

46. Massachusetts is my state, Boston's my city. Here we love to eat grinders, which are "subs" or "heroes" to other folks. Add a cone with jimmies and a bottle of tonic from the spa. That's a wicked good meal!

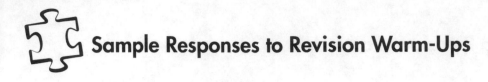

Sample Responses to Revision Warm-Ups

47. Whoosh. That's the sound I heard over and over last night as the basketball magically fell into the hoop each time I shot it. My teammates gawked at my newfound skill. Frankly, I hadn't been playing that well up until last night. But then, every time I took a shot—nothing but net! I played the entire 32 minutes, breathing hard, but playing my heart out. It was as if I was under a spell—a miraculous night when this normally gawky kid was, for all the world, the next Kobe Bryant.

48. (bland, uninteresting voice) Teacher, Don't load down kids like me with so much stuff. Don't assign so much homework. Don't assign more than one or two books per night. Thank you.

Using Strong Verbs

49. I'm traveling by train to my grandma's house. We'll go shopping and lunching every day. She'll braid my hair and while away the hours regaling me with stories about the olden days.

50. Fire ants inflict a fiery sting, which causes a small blister to form after several hours. The blisters itch while healing, and if broken, they can infect the surrounding area, causing severe inflammation and irritation.

51. A distant roar. The rattle of a train track. The swirling sounds of debris. The impending tornado rumbled through the neighborhood, unleashing its fury on trees, fences, and everything in its path. I sat crouched in the corner of the basement, wishing and hoping it would end soon.

52. Savor the flavor of the delicious fruit we call the banana. Chopped down from the banana tree too soon, the fruit tastes bland and bitter. But allowed to ripen, bananas taste sweet, leaving a delightful honey flavor lingering in your mouth long after you've consumed one.

Using Striking Words and Phrases

53. Huddled safely in my bed, I could hear the wild-as-a-coyote howling wind as it blew through the tall pine trees. As I breathed in the night air, it felt thick, almost suffocating, while I waited, trembling, for the inevitable thunderstorm to break.

54. We can expect monumental changes in our environment if the gloomy predictions about global warming turn out to be true. And they seem to be true, indeed, since ice caps are melting, raising the oceans to precarious levels.

55. Watch out for the chicken nuggets! You can fling them across the lunchroom like miniature missiles, knocking out any hapless victim who might accidentally be in the way. These rock-hard, choke-'em-down-if-you-dare morsels make much better weapons than luncheon fare. Trust me—I've tried them both ways.

56. Smack. Squish. Slop. That's what it sounds like when my little brother is eating bananas. I think it is disgusting that he chews with his mouth open, because you can see the smooshed bananas. It's not a pretty sight. It's revolting, repulsive, and repugnant. In fact, it's a most disgusting thing to be around, but no matter how much I protest, he does it anyway.

Using Words That Are Specific and Accurate

57. Butterflies are beautiful flying insects with large scaly wings. The largest butterfly in the world is the female Queen Alexandra's birdwing butterfly. It lives in New Guinea and has a wingspan of up to 12.5 inches. The smallest butterfly is the western pygmy blue. It has a wingspan of only 0.62 inches; it's really tiny. Monarch butterflies migrate over 2,000 miles, flying from Canada to central Mexico in the fall, a journey that takes up to three months every year.

58. Even if you are a grommet and you've never surfed before, you can learn to do some pretty amazing things with a surfboard and some gnarly waves. Just remember to hang ten, keeping all your toes over the nose. Even if you get into that heavy surf, you'll be cranking and having a ball as you barrel into the center of the wave and ride it out.

59. Bridey is a one-in-a-million friend. When she calls me, I know it's her right away when I hear, "Hey you! Get up. It's Saturday morning and we're burning daylight." Even if I'm so sleepy I can hardly keep my eyes open, I get right up so we can hang out at the mall together. Our favorite place is the food court, where she orders a piping-hot chili cheese dog with all the trimmings, and I get double pepperoni pizza with extra-gooey cheese.

60. Chock-full of vitamins, the delicious yellow fruit called the banana gives the body potassium and energy. In fact, two bananas can give you enough energy for a 30-minute workout. Bananas can relieve heartburn and calm frazzled nerves, and when rubbed on a mosquito bite, they can even stop the sting and the itch. Bananas are a handy fruit to have around for lots of reasons.

Using Language Effectively

61. What can I say about Mieka except she's the perfect locker partner? When I have extra books and homework, she never says a thing but moves her stuff to make more room for mine. She decorates with pictures of all my favorite rock stars, and best of all, she doesn't leave a stinky lunch in the locker for days on end like my last locker partner did!

62. A lioness, starved and hungry after days on the African savanna without even a morsel to eat, stalks a herd of caribou migrating north. Spotting the weakest one in the herd, the lioness sneaks up, weaves and bobs her way through the herd, until she can grab one of the legs of the unsuspecting prey and bring it down. With a quick slash to the neck, she kills the caribou, and dinner is finally ready for the lioness, her mate, and their young cubs.

63. As I walked into the most famous room of the Louvre, I experienced the odd sensation of being watched—even laughed at. I turned, and out of the corner of my eye, I saw her. I saw her smile. I caught a glimpse of that magical, mercurial smile that makes the *Mona Lisa* one of the most notable and remarkable paintings in the world. Now, when I face her, the smile fades away and she becomes mysteriously aloof again, tucking away her secrets to be revealed another day.

64. Bananas do so much for your body that it makes sense to eat this nutritious fruit on a regular basis. They are easy to take along in a backpack or in a sack lunch, and when it's time for a midday snack—voilà!—you have your banana ready to peel and eat. Everyone should consider adding bananas to their diet to stay healthy and to have a yummy fruit snack when they get hungry.

Crafting Well-Built Sentences

65. Finally, my two pointy front teeth fell out. They'd been dangling by a thread for the last couple of days, so I knew it was going to happen any minute. Crack. One fell out and then the next. I have two new holes in my mouth where my teeth used to be. And tonight? Who knows? Maybe the tooth fairy will pay me a visit.

66. Exercise gives you energy, helps work off stress, and makes your body stronger. And there are lots of ways to exercise, so everyone should be able to find one that is convenient. Do you like to go to the gym? Great. There are new gyms in most neighborhoods. Prefer the privacy of your bedroom? With a few simple pieces of equipment, you'll be all set. With so much to gain and nothing to lose (but a few extra pounds), it's time to start your own exercise plan today.

67. When you have the flu you feel awful. You can't sleep and you are restless. Every inch of your body aches and you can't remember the last time you could keep any food down. "Get away from me!" is what you want to scream at everyone who offers to help. About the only thing that makes you feel better is a cool washcloth on your forehead and your own soft, cushiony pillow. Ahh, sleep. Please. Let me sleep away this terrible flu.

68. You can begin playing soccer when you are as young as 5 or 6 years old, and continue playing well into your adult life. For many people, it's a lifelong sport. All around the world people play soccer and enjoy it as players and as spectators, too. If you've never played soccer or been to a soccer game, you should change that. Soccer is the best.

Varying Sentence Patterns

69. For the last few years, my family has done the same thing on every vacation. To be perfectly honest, it's getting boring. I wish we could fly somewhere instead of driving. Now, that would be awesome. Or, if we did drive, maybe we could drive straight there instead of stopping at every last rest stop and scenic point between our house and my grandparents'. It would be much faster. And we'd be in better moods when we got there. Good idea!

70. Rainy days don't have to be a washout. There are lots of fun things to do that will keep you happy for hours. For instance, try writing a play. It can be about anything you want. Have you dreamed of being a pirate on the high seas? Or an astronaut exploring a new galaxy in your spaceship? Figure out the characters, then rummage through old boxes of toys and clothes and pick out costumes for your play. Use your imagination. It's always there to have fun with, even on a rainy day.

71. Imagine holding up a big trombone, blowing in the mouthpiece, and manipulating the slider so each note comes out perfectly. It took a lot of work to get to this point, but there's nothing like playing a musical instrument when you can nail the notes to a song. Ba-room. You lean into the trombone and blow with all your might. All those years of practice really paid off, just like your mom and dad promised. You grin as you continue to play, thinking, "Hey world, look at me now."

72. Kerplump! That's the sound you make when you head butt the ball in soccer. It's not an easy thing to learn, but when you use your head (get it?), then you have a better chance to do well on the soccer field.

Breaking the "Rules" to Create Fluency

73. Crunch! Crash! That's what you hear when you go walking in the woods with my friend Tim. He's not very good at walking lightly through the forest. Not at all. If you want to see any animals while you walk, don't go with Tim. They run when they hear him coming. He might as well yell out, "Hello, out there! Here I come!"

74. Have you ever thought to yourself, "Man, I wish I'd bought the comfortable athletic shoes instead of these trendy-looking ones. Ouch! I shoulda listened to my mom." Comfort and construction. Those are two things everyone should consider when buying new athletic shoes. Those new hip shoes may look great, but when your feet are screaming "Take them off!" you should listen and buy sensible, comfortable shoes next time. Trust me. Trust your mom.

75. Remember being afraid of the dark when you were little? I do. I remember it vividly. Every single noise in the house terrified me, from the creaking of the hot and cold water pipes to the rattle of the window by the wind. Thump! I'd run to the safety of the closet when our old tomcat jumped off the sofa and padded out to the kitchen for a snack. I'd cower in there until finally—many hours later—my mom would find me. "What in the world?" she'd ask. And I'd grin at her, so glad, so very glad I survived the night and was ready to come out and enjoy the day.

Sample Responses to Revision Warm-Ups

76. "Run faster! Run harder!" That's what my soccer coach yells at me during practice. But inside my head I hear, "Whoa! Stop!" My heart is pounding, and my lungs are gulping down the air. Practice is hard work for me, but it's all paying off. We're winning some games! Since we started running more and learning new plays, our team has beaten three of our toughest opponents. Way to go, team!

Capturing a Smooth and Rhythmic Flow

77. My cat is the most amazing creature. Part cat, part dog, she likes to follow you wherever you go. If you lean down close, she will lick your face and hand with her sandpaper tongue. It may sound sweet, but honestly? It doesn't feel too great. Sometimes I think my cat is part human, too. When I'm not feeling well, it's as though she understands because she sleeps on my bed with me, keeping my feet warm and cozy. My kitty is the best, the very best in the world.

78. Is there any kid out there who likes to do chores? Probably not. But as boring as chores are, they have to get done. One trick is to get them done quickly, and then you don't have to think about them the rest of the day. Another idea is to make up little games while you do your chores, like pretending you are from another planet and everything in the trash is new and unknown to you. As you gather the trash from throughout the house, try to figure out what everything is and what it is used for. See? Chores can be more fun than you think.

79. When you dance, try to think only about the music and the rhythm of the beat. If you relax your body and feel the music way down deep inside, you'll begin to sway with it naturally. Move to the steps of the dance—waltz, tango, fox-trot, or swing—embracing the music as you look into the eyes of your partner and enjoy the sensation of dancing together in perfect harmony. With practice you'll begin to dance so naturally that you won't even have to think about the direction or number of steps. Until then, let the music lead the way and dance.

80. (boring, lacking fluency) You are at the championship soccer game for your school. You are the goalie, a difficult position. You've practiced hard. You are ready for the biggest game of your life. You watch the other players get the ball and run down toward the goal. You are in the goal. You are waiting for them to try to make a goal. You have a very important job on the team as the goalie. You grab the ball as the other team kicks It toward the goal. You stop the other team from scoring. You are the hero of the game. You are happy.

Answers to Editing Warm-Ups

SPELLING

81. I(beleive)the pie Ray and I ate was cherry rhubarb, but(niether)of us is sure.

I believe the pie Ray and I ate was cherry rhubarb, but neither of us is sure.

82. My(nieghbor's)(condieted)(neice)thought her cookies were better than mine.

My neighbor's conceited niece thought her cookies were better than mine.

83. My best(freind)was so full, she took a(breif)run to get some(releif.)

My best friend was so full, she took a brief run to get some relief.

84. The(wieght)of the cake I carried was so burdensome that I had to(iether)(sieze)it with both hands or let it drop.

The weight of the cake I carried was so burdensome that I had to either seize it with both hands or let it drop.

85. To my(releif,)the casheir put a(reciept)in the bag for the donuts I bought.

To my relief, the cashier put a receipt in the bag for the donuts I bought.

86. The map shows red lines,(signifiing)Canada's(boundarys.)

The map shows red lines, signifying Canada's boundaries.

87. (Ordinaryly,)U.S. citizens must present a passport to(temporaryly)stay in Canada.

Ordinarily, U.S. citizens must present a passport to temporarily stay in Canada.

88. "Will customs take long?" Mom(worryed.)"Not more than an hour," I(replyed.)

"Will customs take long?" Mom worried. "Not more than an hour," I replied.

89. A passport stamp(signifys)that you have successfully met the expectations of the Canadian immigration(authoritys)and may enter the country.

A passport stamp signifies that you have successfully met the expectations of the Canadian immigration authorities and may enter the country.

90. I liked the(orderlyness)of the(communitys)I visited in Canada.

I liked the orderliness of the communities I visited in Canada.

Answers to Editing Warm-Ups

SPELLING

91. The athlete admited that he had stoped short of the finish line.

The athlete admitted that he had stopped short of the finish line.

92. The weter the track became, the more danger it posed for the runer

The wetter the track became, the more danger it posed for the runner.

93. The runer felt robed of his chance to break the course record.

The runner felt robbed of his chance to break the course record.

94. He returnned to the gym in a foul mood, admiting his disappointment.

He returned to the gym in a foul mood, admitting his disappointment.

95. The coach reminded him that rain occured often in the spring and he should not worry about controling it.

The coach reminded him that rain occurred often in the spring and he should not worry about controlling it.

96. I am hopful that my garden is becomeing lush and colorful.

I am hopeful that my garden is becoming lush and colorful.

97. Prepareing soil makes me grimey, but I enjoy scrapeing dirt into buckets.

Preparing soil makes me grimy, but I enjoy scraping dirt into buckets.

98. I find myself hopeing these slimey slugs will be eaten by birds.

I find myself hoping these slimy slugs will be eaten by birds.

99. The largeest rock over there is becomeing a problem in this lovly garden.

The largest rock over there is becoming a problem in this lovely garden.

100. If my garden continus to grow this well, I would be wasteing my time doing anything other than learning how to be a fameous gardener.

If my garden continues to grow this well, I would be wasting my time doing anything other than learning how to be a famous gardener.

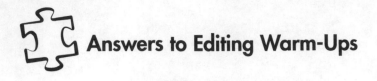

Answers to Editing Warm-Ups

PUNCTUATION

101. The space shuttle is the most complex machine ever made⊙

The space shuttle is the most complex machine ever made.

102. Who would have imagined that space shuttle astronauts would work on the International Space Station as it orbits around the Earth⌃**?**

Who would have imagined that space shuttle astronauts would work on the International Space Station as it orbits around the Earth?

103. How thrilling to see the Earth gradually growing smaller on the horizon⌃**!**

How thrilling to see the Earth gradually growing smaller on the horizon!

104. "I want to become an astronaut," Franklin announced to his parents⊙

"I want to become an astronaut," Franklin announced to his parents.

105. Wow⌃**!** Imagine how exciting it would be to float weightless in space⊙

Wow! Imagine how exciting it would be to float weightless in space.

106. When I go to the movies, I always get popcorn⌃ candy⌃ and a soda.

When I go to the movies, I always get popcorn, candy, and a soda.

107. My favorite kind of pizza has olives⌃ artichokes⌃ sausage⌃ and extra cheese on top.

My favorite kind of pizza has olives, artichokes, sausage, and extra cheese on top.

108. After school I have to walk the dog⌃ take out the trash⌃ and do my homework.

After school I have to walk the dog, take out the trash, and do my homework.

109. Of all the things my little sister does to bug me, breaking my toys⌃ hanging out in my room⌃ and tattling to Mom and Dad are the most annoying.

Of all the things my little sister does to bug me, breaking my toys, hanging out in my room, and tattling to Mom and Dad are the most annoying.

110. I've lived in three countries: Mexico⌃ India⌃ and the United States.

I've lived in three countries: Mexico, India, and the United States.

Answers to Editing Warm-Ups

PUNCTUATION

111. The scorpion's stinger is in its tail.

The scorpion's stinger is in its tail.

112. They're nocturnal, so you're pretty safe from scorpions during the day.

They're nocturnal, so you're pretty safe from scorpions during the day.

113. My school's Spider Club was formed last year by spider fans who wanted to learn all about scorpions' unusual habits.

My school's Spider Club was formed last year by spider fans who wanted to learn all about scorpions' unusual habits.

114. Little has changed about the scorpion's appearance in the last 300 million years.

Little has changed about the scorpion's appearance in the last 300 million years.

115. It's fascinating to learn that scorpions' heads have four to twelve sets of eyes.

It's fascinating to learn that scorpions' heads have four to twelve sets of eyes.

116. "Brrrrr," Mary Sue shivered. "It's the coldest day of the year."

"Brrrrr," Mary Sue shivered. "It's the coldest day of the year."

117. "I'm turning up the heat this instant. It's freezing in here," she said.

"I'm turning up the heat this instant. It's freezing in here," she said.

118. The newspaper's headline announced, "Prepare for Below-Zero Temperatures!"

The newspaper's headline announced, "Prepare for Below-Zero Temperatures!"

119. Mary Sue shook her head, muttering, "I'm not stepping out of this house until spring."

Mary Sue shook her head, muttering, "I'm not stepping out of this house until spring."

120. "I can hardly wait for summer and warm weather," said Mary Sue to her friend Denise on the phone. "We're going to have so much fun at the beach."

"I can hardly wait for summer and warm weather," said Mary Sue to her friend Denise on the phone. "We're going to have so much fun at the beach."

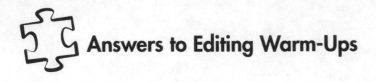

Answers to Editing Warm-Ups

CAPITALIZATION

121. in music class this week, i am going to learn how to play the guitar.

In music class this week, I am going to learn how to play the guitar.

122. how am i ever going to learn all of these chords for the guitar?

How am I ever going to learn all of these chords for the guitar?

123. i've been practicing a lot, so i'm really getting the hang of playing guitar.

I've been practicing a lot, so I'm really getting the hang of playing guitar.

124. one day i hope to become a famous guitar player; i'll travel the world and entertain people everywhere.

One day I hope to become a famous guitar player; I'll travel the world and entertain people everywhere.

125. a famous guitarist whom i admire a lot is Stevie Ray Vaughan.

A famous guitarist whom I admire a lot is Stevie Ray Vaughan.

126. mr. and mrs. Sanchez sent an rsvp to attend our wildlife fund raiser.

Mr. and Mrs. Sanchez sent an RSVP to attend our wildlife fund raiser.

127. I also heard from dr. Turner and governor Yee, who offered to help us.

I also heard from Dr. Turner and Governor Yee, who offered to help us.

128. The manatee is on the endangered species list of the epa in Tallahassee, fl.

The manatee is on the endangered species list of the EPA in Tallahassee, FL.

129. I'll share research about the manatee habitat from professor Morrison of fsu.

I'll share research about the manatee habitat from Professor Morrison of FSU.

130. The Florida Fish and Wildlife Conservancy (fwc) has appointed ms. Lucas and Ed Thomas, jr., to be on the state fund-raising committee to save the manatee.

The Florida Fish and Wildlife Conservancy (FWC) has appointed Ms. Lucas and Ed Thomas, Jr., to be on the state fund-raising committee to save the manatee.

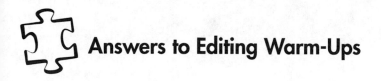

Answers to Editing Warm-Ups

CAPITALIZATION

131. My favorite book of all time is <u>hatchet</u> by Gary Paulsen.

My favorite book of all time is <u>Hatchet</u> by Gary Paulsen.

132. <u>lord of the rings</u> was a very popular book but an even more popular movie.

<u>Lord of the Rings</u> was a very popular book but an even more popular movie.

133. When I was little, my favorite story was "goldilocks and the three bears."

When I was little, my favorite story was "Goldilocks and the Three Bears."

134. On Saturdays, I can't wait to watch looney tunes cartoons.

On Saturdays, I can't wait to watch Looney Tunes cartoons.

135. The best piece of writing that I worked on this year was a story called "the amazing, marvelous, fantastic homework machine."

The best piece of writing that I worked on this year was a story called "The Amazing, Marvelous, Fantastic Homework Machine."

136. This summer we're taking a road trip to visit aunt lanelle in california.

This summer we're taking a road trip to visit Aunt Lanelle in California.

137. We'll go through kansas, colorado, nevada, and new mexico and even stop in arizona to see the grand canyon.

We'll go through Kansas, Colorado, Nevada, and New Mexico and even stop in Arizona to see the Grand Canyon.

138. uncle frank will be there, but my dad's sister vonda will be out of town.

Uncle Frank will be there, but my dad's sister Vonda will be out of town.

139. I hope we can go to disneyland and knott's berry farm while we're in southern california.

I hope we can go to Disneyland and Knott's Berry Farm while we're in Southern California.

140. Let's ask mom to stop at the nevada museum of gold mines in carson city.

Let's ask Mom to stop at the Nevada Museum of Gold Mines in Carson City.

Answers to Editing Warm-Ups

GRAMMAR AND USAGE

141. When you go to Washington, D.C., their are many things to see they're.

When you go to Washington, D.C., there are many things to see there.

142. Visiting a monument? I advice you to stand stationery and take in the cite.

Visiting a monument? I advise you to stand stationary and take in the site.

143. Whose to know how many tourists visit? No one, accept the park service.

Who's to know how many tourists visit? No one, except the park service.

144. I was to overcome with awe to notice too of the smaller side exhibits.

I was too overcome with awe to notice two of the smaller side exhibits.

145. You're favorite monument might be different than mine, but your entitled to you own choice.

Your favorite monument might be different than mine, but you're entitled to your own choice.

146. Last summer I ~~have~~ **had** a part-time job, but it ~~is~~ **was** hard work and ~~takes~~ **took** a lot of time.

Last summer I had a part-time job, but it was hard work and took a lot of time.

147. Jobs like baby-sitting builds self-confidence and develops self-esteem.

Jobs like baby-sitting build self-confidence and develop self-esteem.

148. When you wanted to buy CDs, clothes, or other items, you ~~are needing~~ your own spending money.

When you want to buy CDs, clothes, or other items, you need your own spending money.

149. To getting a good job, you need to has **ve** a good personality and been a good worker.

To get a good job, you need to have a good personality and be a good worker.

150. Everything you did in life can leads **o** to success if you tries **y** 100 percent.

Everything you do in life can lead to success if you try 100 percent.

Answers to Editing Warm-Ups

GRAMMAR AND USAGE

151. Stars are billion~~'~~s and billion~~'~~s of mile~~'~~s away.

Stars are billions and billions of miles away.

152. I found a Web site where you can name a star after yourself: Joseph͗s star. Who wouldn͗t want to do that?

I found a Web site where you can name a star after yourself: Joseph's star. Who wouldn't want to do that?

153. It͗s hard to imagine how we could travel fast enough to reach the stars~~'~~.

It's hard to imagine how we could travel fast enough to reach the stars.

154. At night, I watch for moving star~~'~~s; those are actually satellite~~'~~s.

At night, I watch for moving stars; those are actually satellites.

155. Of all the star~~'~~s, I like the sun the most because it͗s the brightest.

Of all the stars, I like the sun the most because it's the brightest.

156. My female cat Bailey, ~~what~~ _who_ is orange with white stripes, enjoys lying in the sun on ~~his~~ _her_ back.

My female cat Bailey, who is orange with white stripes, enjoys lying in the sun on her back.

157. Laura, the girl ~~what~~ _who_ is going to feed my cat while I am gone, is going to come over on ~~its~~ _her_ way to school each day.

Laura, the girl who [or that] is going to feed my cat while I am gone, is going to come over on her way to school each day.

158. Bailey steals my brother's toys and hides ~~it~~ _them_ where ~~he~~ _they_ can't be found.

Bailey steals my brother's toys and hides them where they can't be found.

159. If you pet ~~it~~ _her_, Bailey rolls over like a dog ~~what~~ _that_ likes ~~their~~ _its_ belly scratched.

If you pet her, Bailey rolls over like a dog that likes its belly scratched.

160. How that cat makes me laugh! I'm glad I have ~~them~~ _her_ to keep my family and ~~I~~ _me_ company.

How that cat makes me laugh! I'm glad I have her to keep my family and me company.

Answers to Editing Warm-Ups

WORKING WITH MULTIPLE CONVENTIONS

161

The fall tv shows this year sounds terific.

There are so many different kinds that I'm sure I'll find a new show who I really like.

Maybe their will be a new Sportscaster who enjoys College football as much as me.

One thing I'm not looking forward to about the fall seeson are all the knew comercials.

it seems as if they're more and more every year.

The fall TV shows this year sound terrific. There are so many different kinds that I'm sure I'll find a new show that I really like. Maybe there will be a new sportscaster who enjoys college football as much as I do. One thing I'm not looking forward to about the fall season is all the new commercials. It seems as if there are more and more every year.

162

One day i timed a half-hour tv show and it were only 19 minuts long after subtracting all the comercials.

It's terible how much time is wastd on comercials.

Most of the time I went to the kitchin to get some thing to eat rather than watch more comerceals.

Their are a few good wons that make you laff.

tv should have more comercials that is entertaning, like those played during the super bowl.

One day I timed a half-hour TV show and it was only 19 minutes long after subtracting all the commercials. It's terrible how much time is wasted on commercials. Most of the time I go to the kitchen to get something to eat rather than watch more commercials. There are a few good ones that make you laugh. TV should have more commercials that are entertaining, like those played during the Super Bowl.

163

when you travel it's hard to find a decent restarant.

There is many places to choose from, but most of it serve fast food, and I'd realy rather have a good hot meel.

It's important to have a helthy meel at the end of a longday in the car with my family.

beleive me, it can be exhausting driveing with them.

One thing I've noticd is that there aren't as many family-stile restarants as fast-food places along the hiway.

Answers to Editing Warm-Ups

When you travel it's hard to find a decent restaurant. There are many places to choose from, but most of them serve fast food, and I'd really rather have a good hot meal. It's important to have a healthy meal at the end of a long day in the car with my family. Believe me, it can be exhausting driving with them. One thing I've noticed is that there aren't as many family-style restaurants as fast-food places along the highway.

164

It culd be that runing and maintaning them is more expensive.
or it could be that there not as poppular with tourists.
Perhaps their hard to find cuz you cant get to them easy from the hiway.
Regardless of the reseon, i still look carfully for a good 1 to eat in with my family.
The rite restarant will hav things we like, and their will be healthy menu choiyces.

It could be that running and maintaining them are more expensive. Or it could be that they're not as popular with tourists. Perhaps they're hard to find because you can't get to them easily from the highway. Regardless of the reason, I still look carefully for a good one to eat in with my family. The right restaurant will have things we like, and there will be healthy menu choices.

165

one of the hardst things about being the youngist in the family is that no 1 thinks me can do anything by myself.
No won beleives that Im old enough to make her own decisions or do anything on her own.
when my older brother want to do things with friends, my Mom and dad say, "sure."
But when I ask to do the same things they say, "no, your to young."
Sometimes I think they were afraid that if they let me make decisions or go out by yourself, they are admiting that their youngest child is growyving up.

One of the hardest things about being the youngest in the family is that no one thinks I can do anything by myself. No one believes that I'm old enough to make my own decisions or do anything on my own. For example, when my older brother wants to do things with friends, my mom and dad say, "Sure." But when I ask to do the same things they say, "No, you're too young." Sometimes I think they are afraid that if they let me make decisions or go out by myself, they are admitting that their youngest child is growing up.

166

My parents definitly don't want to admit that I was growing up.
but it's not fare to me.
I want to have sum fredome, to.
I'd be responsible and show they that I'm worthy, if they'd only give me a chance.
younger kids deserve a chance to does things on his own, two.

My parents definitely don't want to admit that I am growing up. But it's not fair to me. I want to have some freedom, too. I'd be responsible and show them that I'm worthy, if they'd only give me a chance. Younger kids deserve a chance to do things on their own, too.

167

An individual from History I realy admire is abraham lincoln.
he is an intresting person and a Great president, to.
It musta been very hard back in the 1860s to fight aganst all the peopl which wanted to kepe slavery.
But if lincoln hadnt be strong and stood up for his beleifs, we wood not have abolished slavery.
he was the rite man to be President of the united states at the time.

An individual from history I really admire is Abraham Lincoln. He was an interesting person and a great president, too. It must have been very hard back in the 1860s to fight against all the people who wanted to keep slavery. But if Lincoln hadn't been strong and stood up for his beliefs, we would not have abolished slavery. He was the right man to be president of the United States at the time.

168

As a person in today's world, I really admire abraham lincoln becaus he had a hard life.
But he didnt let its problums hold he back.
Comeing from a small town and being very poor when He was young did not stop him from becomeing one of the most important people in american History.
he had a strong caracter and respected peopl as individual's.
his life storey is interesting and enspiring to young people like I.

As a person in today's world, I really admire Abraham Lincoln because he had a hard life. But he didn't let his problems hold him back. Coming from a small town and being very poor when he was young did not stop him from becoming one of the most important people in American history. He had a strong character and respected people as individuals. His life story is interesting and inspiring to young people like me.

Answers to Editing Warm-Ups

169

my parents think I should keeps mine room spotlessly cleen

I disagrae. i sae it's my room and it should bee how I like it.

However, thay make me cleen it ever weak end whether I like it or not

Its not fun at All, let me tell u.

I had to pick up all my clothes, put away my games and toyz, restack my books on the shelfs,

and dust and vacume.

> My parents think I should keep my room spotlessly clean. I disagree. I say it's my room and it should be how I like it. However, they make me clean it every weekend, whether I like it or not. It's not fun at all, let me tell you. I have to pick up all my clothes, put away my games and toys, restack my books on the shelves, and dust and vacuum.

170

then I hav ta wash my sheats and re make my bed

Their is a lot to do every weak end cuz I dont do much during the weak.

What really bugs me is that cents im the oldest, i hav to do the work all by myselves.

My Mom and Dad help my litle brothers and sisters—that's not fare.

Don't tell them I told you this, But when my room is finaly cleen i realy like it.

> Then I have to wash my sheets and remake my bed. There is a lot to do every weekend because I don't do much during the week. What really bugs me is that since I'm the oldest, I have to do the work all by myself. My mom and dad help my little brothers and sisters—that's not fair. Don't tell them I told you this, but when my room is finally clean I really like it.

171

Skatebor, ding can be an Art, a Hobby, a Sport, or just a way to get around conveniently.

some peopl call it a extreem sport because it is so creativ.

In 2002, a report from the marketing research firm american sports data revealed that their were

12.5 million skateboarders in the world.

Eigty percent of those Skateboarders were under the age of 18, & 74 percent is mail.

Skate Boarding are a sport that has really taken of in the last 20 yeers.

> Skateboarding can be an art, a hobby, a sport, or just a way to get around conveniently. Some people call it an extreme sport because it is so creative. In 2002, a report from the marketing research firm American Sports Data revealed that there were 12.5 million skateboarders in the world. Eighty percent of those skateboarders were under the age of 18, and 74 percent were male. Skateboarding is a sport that has really taken off in the last 20 years.

172

The street is the place of choyce for today's Skate boarders.
the boards and wheels are very lite compared to the early verzions.
since the 1990s, tho, skatboards isn't changed that much.
Their are many skate board parks in city's across the countrie where skate boarders can freestyle skate and try out exciting new moves on Ramps and vertical drops.
the Ollie is the basis for many triks, but the Flip was today's most popular move.

The street is the place of choice for today's skateboarders. The boards and wheels are very light compared to the early versions. Since the 1990s, though, skateboards haven't changed that much. There are many skateboard parks in cities across the country where skateboarders can freestyle skate and try out exciting new moves on ramps and vertical drops. The Ollie is the basis for many tricks, but the flip is today's most popular move.

173

1 of the things I'd change at my school is the rule about Not Eating in clas.
i think it is realy hard to sit still all day and not had any thing to eat.
Kids nede snaks to give them Energy 4 learning.
If they're was a time in the morning for snack, for instence, than everyone could have a quik byte, feel better, and be Ready to Learn more right away.
their would have to be rule's abowt witch snaks would work, though.

One of the things I'd change at my school is the rule about not eating in class. I think it is really hard to sit still all day and not have anything to eat. Kids need snacks to give them energy for learning. If there was a time in the morning for snack, for instance, then everyone could have a quick bite, feel better, and be ready to learn more right away. There would have to be rules about which snacks would work, though.

174

For egsample, you couldn't have a Snack that needed refrigeration or heeting.
But you could has a snack like a piece of fruit some cheese and crackers or a Granola Bar.
these kinds of snacks wood be easy to prepare and simple to dispose of when your finished.
Kid's would hat to clean up after Snack Time and not leaves extra food lying around.
It could be fun healthy and an good way to break up the day if we were allowwed to have snack's at school.

Answers to Editing Warm-Ups

For example, you couldn't have a snack that needed refrigeration or heating. But you could have a snack like a piece of fruit, some cheese and crackers, or a granola bar. These kinds of snacks would be easy to prepare and simple to dispose of when you're finished. Kids would have to clean up after snack time and not leave extra food lying around. It could be fun, healthy, and a good way to break up the day if we were allowed to have snacks at school.

175

Becomeing a Teacher is alot of hard work and takes meny years of Study.
They are a wonderful job, however, cuz you get to help kids lern
what culd possibly be moore rewarding then that?
Although their are many difficult things to learn to be a good Teacher, its a very worthwhile Profession.
helping a New Generation learn how to read & rite is an awesome responsibility and alot of fun, to

Becoming a teacher is a lot of hard work and takes many years of study. It is a wonderful job, however, because you get to help kids learn. What could possibly be more rewarding than that? Although there are many difficult things to learn to be a good teacher, it's a very worthwhile profession. Helping a new generation learn how to read and write is an awesome responsibility and a lot of fun, too.

176

What would you wants to do if you where a teacher?
Id want to teach art, and paint from september to joon.
My students will probably like to work with clay, collage, and printmaking, too
Sculptur in 3 dimensions would be one of many exsiting activitys.
I bet he culd build the Brooklyn bridge from woodin sticks and gloo.

What would you want to do if you were a teacher? I'd want to teach art, and paint from September to June. My students would probably like to work with clay, collage, and printmaking, too. Sculpture in three dimensions would be one of many exciting activities. I bet they could build the Brooklyn Bridge from wooden sticks and glue.

Answers to Editing Warm-Ups

177

were
last year there was two earthquakes you could really feel in san Francisco.
I know because my friend's cusin lives their.
She calls california the shake-n-bake state because they are so many earthquakes and it
is
was so hot.
have   u   y're
buildings has to be bilt to a special code to make sure their stable.
Otherwise, they'll just crumbled into dust.

Last year there were two earthquakes you could really feel in San Francisco. I know because my friend's cousin lives there. She calls California the shake-n-bake state because there are so many earthquakes and it is so hot. Buildings have to be built to a special code to make sure they're stable. Otherwise, they'll just crumble into dust.

178

e
I am greatful that I live far away from they're, but we're still in a quake zone.
I   c   e
Me and my dad have practiced earthquake drills by hideing in the bathtub or standing in a
y o
sturdie doorway.
f
It's not save to go outside during an Earthquake, even if you wants to get away from the bilding.
o
if you are at schol durring an earthquake, you should take cover under you're desk.
i   n   #
You should always have lots of fresh water, a radeo, and caned food ready incase of an
emergency.

I am grateful that I live far away from there, but we're still in a quake zone. My dad and I have practiced earthquake drills by hiding in the bathtub or standing in a sturdy doorway. It's not safe to go outside during an earthquake, even if you want to get away from the building. If you are at school during an earthquake, you should take cover under your desk. You should always have lots of fresh water, a radio, and canned food ready in case of an emergency.

179

h
It's so hard togo to bed wen my parents tell me too.
i try hard to fall asleep, but it's not easy when it's still light out or when im not tyred
hide   i
Sometimes I hid a book under the covers and read later in to the nyght.
hear   c
I turns the light out really fast if I here my Mom or dad comming to chek on me.
l   y   e
with the covers puled up, I try to breathe normaly until them have left the room, and than I go
back to reading until I fall asleep.

Answers to Editing Warm-Ups

It's so hard to go to bed when my parents tell me to. I try hard to fall asleep but it's not easy when it's still light out or when I'm not tired. Sometimes I hide a book under the covers and read late into the night. I turn the light out really fast if I hear my mom or dad coming to check on me. With the covers pulled up, I try to breathe normally until they have left the room, and then I go back to reading until I fall asleep.

180

in addition to new bedtime rules, their should be a rule againgst home work.
if you work really hard at school all day, you shouldnt have to do moore work at home.
Two much homework could makke you're brane so tired they mite wear out.
if all you do are homework everie night, you don't had enuf time to play outside with
you're friends.
Kids shouldn't have to much work to do at home because then they wont get to due all the
fun things that are good for them todo.

In addition to new bedtime rules, there should be a rule against homework. If you work really hard at school all day, you shouldn't have to do more work at home. Too much homework could make your brain so tired it might wear out. If all you do is homework every night, you don't have enough time to play outside with your friends. Kids shouldn't have too much work to do at home because then they won't get to do all the fun things that are good for them to do.

Notes